THE

AFTER WORK

COOK

THE
AFTER WORK
COOK

by

Maggie Brogan

PAPERFRONTS
ELLIOT RIGHT WAY BOOKS
KINGSWOOD, SURREY, U.K.

Typeset in 10pt on 11pt by One & A Half Graphics, Redhill, Surrey. Made and Printed in Great Britain by Richard Clay Ltd., Bungay, Suffolk.

DEDICATION

To After Work Cooks everywhere, especially those
who parted with their own favourite quickie recipes
for inclusion in the book.

CONTENTS

1 INTRODUCTION

More than ever before men and women are having to juggle the demands of work and home. Whether they are wives and mothers, divorcees bringing up children single-handed, lone fathers, people living alone or working couples, thousands are forced to limit their culinary skills to a frantic 30 minutes each evening.

Statistically, women still do the most cooking, with men more likely to eat out, buy ready-made meals or rely on the local pizza delivery service. Even so, there has been a marked rise in the number of men who enjoy rustling up an interesting meal, either for themselves and friends or for their families. These recipes are designed to be high on taste and low on hassle for those whose lives are too short to spend much time in the kitchen.

As a home economist I have always been amused, and perhaps a little intrigued, at the way some men cook. Most love to experiment, throwing together a dollup of this and a handful of that in the hope that they produce a creative masterpiece. Which they usually do — and in whistle-stop time too! After several years as a working wife and mother I realise that subconsciously men have taught me a thing or two about cooking in a hurry.

Cooking is not a strict science and need not be confined to a straitjacket of do's and don'ts and must's and must not's. Allow your own personality and instinct to intrude into a recipe. Don't worry too much about weighing or measuring ingredients, rely instead, as all good cooks do, on taste.

According to a survey recently carried out by the University of Newcastle, the whole pattern of the way people eat is changing. No longer does traditional family life revolve around meat and two veg served at the same time each day.

The survey reports that the average time spent preparing meals is less than 10 minutes and members of the family often eat at different times. Lap meals in front of the television have become perfectly acceptable and convenience food is no longer the mark of a lazy individual.

Research also shows that many women actually prefer to spend their time working, pursuing hobbies and doing things with family and friends rather than trudging the eternal triangle of cooker, sink and dining table, and family life is benefiting say the experts.

After a long tiring day, often thinking of what to cook presents the biggest problem. Sometimes we want to eat something which is nice and tasty but a bit different from a grilled chop and boiled vegetables. The last thing we want to do is spend precious time searching for a recipe which doesn't demand hours of slogging. All too often we end up reaching for the sausages or beefburgers and dragging out the chip pan.

Yet fast need not mean junk. By all means be choosy about convenience foods but don't feel guilty about using those which you can make work for you. Match the best of the manufactured with the choicest fresh ingredients.

Jam, bread, canned soup and even butter, are convenience foods yet they have been around so long we don't view them as such. Ready-made products like pastry, packet sauces, instant potato, pasta, canned beans and vegetables are just a few convenience foods which are ideal in helping prepare a quick meal.

Of course there are some excellent commercially prepared meals on the market. The array of exotic-sounding names like Tagliatelle Vegetali and Caribbean Chicken are indeed tempting, but costly if you are catering for more than one. Surprisingly perhaps, it is quite quick and simple, and considerably cheaper, to make similar dishes yourself.

How do you define quick and simple? Views may differ. My idea is to avoid recipes which demand too much fiddly preparation, although inevitably there must be some. And I hate having to use too many utensils, saucepans and dishes. Trying to re-create the banqueting department of the Savoy Hotel is not my idea of a stress-free evening!

This book aims to use as few ingredients as possible, and eliminate too much weighing and measuring. To cut down time spent shopping, most — if not all — of the ingredients are available from larger supermarkets.

Most of the recipes featured can be prepared and cooked within 30 to 40 minutes, and in some cases even less. Also included are a few which are simple to prepare but take longer to cook. Sometimes, once a load of ingredients has been thrown into a pot, it's nice to relax with a glass of wine while a meal bubbles away in the oven.

Unfortunately, quick often means expensive. Some of the dishes would certainly do justice to a dinner party, but most people have to stretch their financial resources so there are plenty of economical ideas too.

You can for instance make a quick and cheap sauce for pasta by frying a sliced onion and some crushed garlic in a little oil, adding a can of chopped tomatoes, a few bruised leaves of oregano and a dash or two of Tabasco sauce then topping with a generous dusting of Parmesan cheese. The result? A family meal for half the price of this book!

Depending on budget, the same sauce can be made more exotic with the addition of thinly sliced peppered salami, a few black olives, a handful of button mushrooms and a splash of red wine. In no time you can serve a meal fit for the most discerning connoisseur!

This book aims, not just to give recipes but to stimulate the imagination and encourage improvisation. A book to dip into perhaps — an ideas book.

When you think about it, all recipes are just a variation on a theme. It is the way in which ingredients are combined, the contrast in textures and blending of flavours and colours, which give each dish its own unique taste and appearance.

Experiment and have fun. Use the recipes as a basic guide, adding or substituting favourite ingredients until you create a dish to your own personal satisfaction.

2   WHAT'S IN STORE?

Dashing to the shops a few minutes before closing time for the odd item missing from a recipe does nothing to relieve the stress of after work cooking. A frantic ten minutes in the lunch hour, or a three mile drive to the late-night grocer isn't much good either.

In an ideal world we would sit down for half an hour on a Sunday evening, plan our menus for the week and shop once for all the goods. But for most of us life just isn't that organised.

Concocting a meal becomes infinitely quicker if a range of versatile and non-perishable ingredients are to hand. A well-stocked store cupboard alleviates the stress of cooking when you are too tired, get in late or haven't had time to shop.

Often on such evenings impromptu guests arrive and, having boldly made the suggestion that they stay for supper, panic-stricken you try to visualise what lies lurking in the fridge/cupboard/larder. If you're anything like me it won't be much: a bit of mouldy cheese, half a can of fruit cocktail and a jar of mincemeat your mother made years ago! It won't do your reputation as a cook much good and you end up suggesting a take-away.

Vow to change things now! Actually in order to write this book I have been forced to follow my own instructions and have been amazed how much easier and quicker after work cooking can be.

Keeping at least some of the items listed in this chapter, tucked away in a cupboard, really does save time, energy and hassle.

Time spent shopping is drastically reduced because you only have to shop for fresh produce. Non-perishables can be replaced gradually which spreads the cost. Contrary to popular belief it is possible to eat nothing but dried, canned and frozen food and remain in perfect health.

Grains, pasta and pulses, which have a shelf life of six to 12 months, offer unlimited scope for knocking up quick and tasty meals. Often the simplest is the nicest. Try tossing a chunk of butter and some finely chopped garlic through freshly cooked tagliatelle and sprinkle liberally with Parmesan cheese.

Canned vegetables, fish and meat last in good condition for about one year provided they are stored correctly, i.e. in a cool, dry cupboard. Experiment with different combinations and various dressings, to make interesting salads.

Try a mixture of chick peas, red-brown beans, sliced artichoke hearts and sweet red peppers. Toss through a couple of tablespoons of dark and spicy dressing (see page 57). For added substance and flavour, crumble over some feta cheese (which has a fridge-life of two months) or flaked tuna fish and a few black olives. Keep a packet of melba toast in the cupboard to serve with this type of salad.

Beans, lentils and rice can also be thrown together with a variety of herbs, spices and fresh vegetables to make tasty meals. (See chapter 6 on Pasta, Grains and Pulses.)

Cans of tomatoes are indispensable to the cook in a hurry. Several varieties are now available, including those with onion and chilli. Chopped tomatoes are useful for making all manner of sauce bases for meat, fish, pasta and vegetables. Even a simple sauce can lift an otherwise plain dish into something really brilliant.

It is worth keeping a few sun-dried tomatoes in stock. These are fairly expensive and not that easy to find but because of their strong taste a few go a long way. Use them in salads as a stand-by, or smeared on pitta bread as a base for pizza-type toppings.

Stuffing mixes make ideal crunchy toppings and add taste and bulk to fish and vegetable dishes. With none of the chore of making breadcrumbs, varieties include apple, herb and garlic and herb and apricot as well as the traditional favourites.

Try brushing some lamb cutlets with beaten egg and then drop them one by one into a small polythene bag filled with parsley and thyme stuffing mix. Give the bag a shake and then simply remove the chops and cook them under the grill.

Indian naan bread is another good stand-by. Although the dough needs proving for an hour, so little work is involved. You simply roll it out and pop under the grill. The result is a deliciously scorched and puffy outside and a soft moist inside. Naan bread makes a good accompaniment to pulse and vegetable casseroles, stir-fries and kebabs. One packet will serve four people.

Keep a few packets of sauce mixes in stock as well. Hollandaise, with its lemony flavour, is good with fish. I find the cheese mix disappointing and prefer instead to use the basic white and add freshly grated cheese.

Although it's a useful stand-by to keep a few jars of dried herbs in the cupboard, nothing gives life to food more than the flavour of fresh herbs. Supermarkets don't always have a big selection in stock, which is frustrating especially if you have gone there in search of a particular variety.

Herbs are easy to grow and it saves time to keep a pot by the kitchen door. A basic supply includes parsley, chives, sage, thyme, chervil, mint, rosemary, basil and marjoram. All but mint and rosemary can be grown in a multi-planter (a big pot with holes in the side). Mint has invasive roots and should be planted in its own container, and rosemary grows into a bush and therefore needs more space.

Fresh herbs give a welcome 'bite' to dull salads. Try a mix of shredded iceburg lettuce and roughly chopped parsley, mint, chervil, tarragon and coriander. Toss in a well flavoured vinaigrette dressing – delicious!

There is no need to spend time and energy chopping fresh herbs to death. Take a few sprigs and chop just enough to bruise the leaves, thus releasing their aromatic flavour. Toss into dishes at the last minute.

Dried fruit has a shelf life of about three months and canned fruit about one year. Soak a selection overnight – apricots, apple, peaches – and then stew in a little water and demerara sugar until tender. Allow to cool and mix with some of the more exotic canned varieties – lychees, black cherries, melon – and serve with a scoop of good quality ice cream and one or two Continental-style biscuits.

A can of sweetened chestnut purée provides nature's instant dessert — purer and nicer than packets of 'chemical cocktail'. Just spoon the purée into individual glasses and pipe whipped cream around the edge. Again, Continental-style biscuits make a good accompaniment. Or use the purée as a delicious, emergency ice cream topping.

Home Economics is all about knowing what is available to make kitchen life more convenient in a busy life. Shop around and test out some non-perishable foods which may be unfamiliar. Finding your particular favourites and keeping a variety in stock will enable you to prepare lots of interesting meals in the shortest possible time.

Store Cupboard Stock List
Vegetable oil
Olive oil
Sesame seed oil
Vinegar — red wine
　　　　　　white wine
　　　　　　raspberry
Stock cubes
Yeast extract
Worcestershire sauce
Soy sauce
Tabasco sauce
Cranberry sauce
Mustard powder
Mustard seeds
French mustard
Wholegrain mustard
Black peppercorns
Green peppercorns in brine
Salt
Crushed chillies
Chilli powder
Hot pepper or chilli sauce
Mexican chilli seasoning
Cayenne pepper

Paprika pepper
Ground coriander
Coriander seeds
Fenugreek seeds
Sesame seeds
Ground cumin
Ground ginger
Garam masala
Dried mixed herbs
Curry powder
Curry paste
Tomato ketchup
Black olives
Sun-dried tomatoes

CANS
Vegetables — chopped tomatoes
             sweetcorn
             celery
             asparagus
             artichokes
             chick peas
             mushrooms
Beans — red kidney
        aduki
        flageolet
        red-brown
        borlotti
        cannellini
Fish/Meat — Tuna in oil
            Salmon
            Ham
            Corned beef
Soups — condensed mushroom
        condensed tomato rice
        condensed chicken
        cream of tomato
Fruit — Lychees

Black cherries
Mango
Melon
Pineapple chunks
Pineapple rings
Crushed pineapple
Mandarin oranges

Custard (ready made)
Dried fruit — Apricots
Peaches
Apples

DRY FOOD
Pasta — Tagliatelle
Noodles
Spaghetti
Twists/bows/tubes
Cannelloni
Rice — Basmati
Wild
Brown
Saffron
Pillau
Lentils — Red
Green/Continental
Bulgar Wheat
Instant potato
Naan bread mix
Dried mushrooms
Onions
Garlic
Nuts — Walnuts
Flaked almonds
Cashew nuts
Vacuum-packed chestnuts
Packet sauce mixes — White
Onion
Hollandaise
Bolognese

Packet stuffing mixes — Parsley and thyme
                                    Herb and garlic
Chestnut purée
Soft brown sugar
Demerara sugar
Clear honey
Orange marmalade
Lime marmalade
Jams
Golden syrup
Peanut butter
Vanilla essence
Plain chocolate
Gelatine
Flour
Breadcrumbs
Desiccated coconut
Sultanas
Icing sugar
Sponge fingers
Continental-style biscuits — Amaretti
                                    Wafers
                                    Ratafias
                                    Langues du chat
Melba toast

Fridge Stores

Although it is advisable to buy perishable foods regularly, the
fridge can be stocked with a few longer-lasting ingredients which
are useful in knocking up a quick meal.

Cheese: Feta and Parmesan last for several weeks and a tub of
grated Parmesan is especially useful for flavouring pasta meals and
sprinkling over food in a sauce prior to grilling. Cheddar and other
similar hard cheeses last in good condition for a couple of weeks.

Mayonnaise: A jar of French-style mayonnaise, and perhaps one
or two mayonnaise-based dressings are a must. Flavours include

Avocado and Smoked Ham, Mild Curry, Garlic and Herb and Chilli and Avocado. Any one is ideal for turning a mundane salad into a bistro-style extravaganza. (See Avocado and Bacon Salad, page 128).

Eggs: Eggs will keep for about 2 weeks, and half a dozen or so will always provide an instant omelette when time and energy are short.

Suet: Quick tasty casseroles can often be made from a variety of left-overs, or odds and ends of vegetables. A packet of shredded suet is useful to keep in the fridge for adding bulk and interest to such dishes. Vegetarian nut suet is available from health food shops.

Root Ginger: Fresh ginger keeps well in the fridge and is a useful flavouring for stir-fries and desserts.

Vacuum-packed salami and Pepperoni: These highly flavoured cooked meats are wonderful for pizza-type toppings, pasta sauces and snacks.

Tomato purée: Keep a tube tucked away in the fridge. It is indispensable for adding flavour and colour to sauces and casseroles.

Garlic and Herb butter: Again available in tubes it is most useful for tossing through freshly cooked pasta or making your own quick garlic bread.

Jif Lemon: A plastic lemon filled with juice is the answer when there are no fresh lemons in stock. Also less wasteful when a recipe calls for 'a squeeze' of lemon juice.

3   MAKE IT SNAPPY

No matter how simple a recipe is, inevitably there has to be some preparation otherwise it wouldn't be a recipe! And this means time chopping, time grating, time making a salad and time cooking vegetables and other accompaniments to a meal.

There are a few short cuts which can make life easier. Vegetables don't have to be cooked to death. Break the habits of a lifetime and simmer in a little water until just tooth-tender — the French have been doing it for years!

Alternatively don't cook vegetables at all — serve crudités instead. These are a selection of raw crunchy and healthy vegetables such as carrots, celery, cucumber, tomatoes, cauliflower, courgettes, mushrooms, fennel and radishes. Simply cut the vegetables into small florets, matchsticks or slices and either serve plain or trickled with vinaigrette dressing or with a tasty dip.

Crudités make a good accompaniment to many meat and fish dishes and also the type of light suppers featured in the Television Snacks chapter.

When planning meals it saves time and effort if you think in terms of two or three days at a time. Prepare a selection of crudités in one go and store in the fridge in a container with a tight-fitting lid.

Salad greens can be kept in the same way. To prolong the life of lettuce and watercress, cut a sliver off the stalk (watercress can be done a bunch at a time) and hold the head under cold running water for a few seconds. Shake well and store in the fridge.

Don't waste precious minutes boiling away delicate flavours; hours spent in the kitchen are something every after work cook can do without!

The goodness in potatoes lies just beneath the skin, so boil small new potatoes in their jackets. Scrub with a nailbrush rather than scraping or peeling. Bake larger potatoes in the oven or microwave.

Save time by cooking two or three times the number of potatoes you need. On subsequent nights they can be chopped, mixed with finely chopped onion and a little mayonnaise and served cold, or sliced and sautéd.

Extra vegetables can be cooked in the same way and used for dishes like the Vegetable and Cheese Bake (see page 41).

Chopped onion and garlic are common ingredients in quick recipes and again it saves time to prepare a week's supply in one go. Chop a few onions and cloves of garlic but remember that such highly flavoured foods must be stored in containers with tightly fitted lids otherwise all other food in the fridge will be tainted.

Chopped parsley is useful for flavouring and garnish. As it stays fresher and greener than most other herbs, chop a couple of bunches at a time and keep in the fridge. It's a great relief to be able to take out a handful when required, rather than have to chop a little each time a recipe demands a tablespoon or two.

Grated cheese has a multitude of uses and although available ready-grated, it is an expensive way of buying. Instead grate a block of cheese in one go and store in a covered container in the fridge.

Many of the recipes are a complete meal in themselves; others include suggested accompaniments and time should be allowed for their preparation and cooking. Usually this can be done while the main dish is cooking.

4 ABOUT THE RECIPES

In terms of workload and financial restraints, the average woman who is juggling her job with her family is probably the hardest hit by after work cooking. For this reason the recipes — bar one or two — are designed to serve two adults and two children.

Yet there comes a time when even the bed-sit dweller, who relies on take-aways, and the executive who dines out, yearns for a home-cooked meal.

The experienced cook will no doubt work out his or her own ways of adapting the recipes to serve fewer people. Juggling ingredients and gauging quantities comes with experience, or trial and error. As a general guide, the recipes which are the easiest to adapt to single servings are those which won't leave you with loads of left-overs.

Here are some examples:

Mexican Honeyed Chicken (page 118) For a single serving use two or three chicken thighs and make the glaze with 1 tablespoon of honey and half a teaspoon of chilli powder.
Devilled Chicken Drumsticks (page 122) — For a single serving use about two drumsticks and make up the marinade with 1 tablespoon of oil, a shake of paprika and ginger and half a teaspoon

of mustard powder. If, when you come to make the dish again, a more distinctive flavour is preferred, simply add more of the spices.

Eggs Duchesse (page 33) — For a single serving use 2 eggs, 1 tablespoon of milk, 1 tablespoon of dried mushrooms, 1 slice of ham and a knob of butter the size of a hazelnut.

Spaghetti Provençal (page 46) — For a single serving use 1 small onion, 1 courgette, omit the leeks, 1 oz (25g) mushrooms, half a tablespoon of oil, 2-3 oz (50-75g) spaghetti, and substitute the can of tomatoes for 2 chopped fresh tomatoes, a squeeze of tomato purée and a dash of water.

Honey and Mustard Glazed Lamb (page 108) — For a single serving use one lamb chop and a glaze made with half a teaspoon of honey and half a teaspoon of French mustard.

Another way of adapting a recipe is to cook enough of the main ingredient — usually meat, poultry, fish or pasta — to serve one or two people, but stick to the quantities given for the other ingredients. (That way you won't be left with half cans and cartons of perishables which invariably get thrown out.) Put the excess mixture or sauce in a small container and freeze it for future use. Even the ice compartment of a fridge will do. Time and energy are saved, because when you next fancy the same meal, all you have to do is cook the main ingredient.

Recipes which adapt well to this method include Turkey Capparis (page 118), Tandoori Chicken (page 120), Pork Royale (page 99), Tagliatelle in Spicy Tomato Sauce (page 45), Spaghetti Provençal (page 46), Pasta Niçoise (page 47), Spaghetti Bolognese (page 50), Bacon Chops with Creamy Mushrooms (page 94), Gammon Marsala (page 97) and Gammon with Plum Relish (page 98).

If you have a freezer, probably the most hassle-free way of cooking for one is to make up a complete recipe and freeze it in four individual dishes.

People cooking for two can of course halve the recipes exactly, unless they have large appetites in which case it might not be necessary! If you choose a recipe where you will be left with half cans and half cartons etc. look for other recipes which use the same ingredients.

For example:

Monday: Creamy Noodles (page 44) using half a carton of double cream.

Tuesday: Ratatouille (page 32) using half a can tomatoes, half an aubergine and half the peppers.

Wednesday: Pork Royale (page 99) using the other half tomatoes and cream.

Thursday: Liver with Peppercorn Sauce (page 106) using half a carton of soured cream.

Friday: Tagliatelle with Spicy Aubergine (page 48) using the other half aubergine and soured cream.

Saturday: Kebabs using the other half peppers.

People cooking for themselves could also follow this method. Similar juggling can be done with other recipes, e.g. those which use whole fruit or tins of fish when you only need half at a time. By planning out a couple of weeks' meals at a time you need never end up with odd bits and pieces.

To avoid unnecessary and time-consuming weighing, wherever possible, tablespoon (abbreviated tablsp) and teaspoon (abbreviated teasp) measurements are used. As a general guide use rounded spoonfuls, except in the case of flavourings when you may like to add more or less according to personal taste.

Technically there are no strict rules as to whether you use plain or self-raising flour for thickening sauces and gravies. However self-raising may produce a more salty flavour — albeit miniscule — because of the raising agents it contains. I have always used whatever is to hand, with good results, including cornflour and brown flour.

Size 2 eggs are used throughout the book; smaller or larger eggs could be used although proportionately you will end up with slightly less or slightly more mixture.

Recipes are given in both imperial and metric measurements and for accuracy you should be consistent. Preparation and cooking times are approximate. Human nature, being what it is, means that some people work quicker than others; oven temperatures too can vary considerably.

Glossary of Culinary Terms

Basmati Rice — a rice grown at the foot of the Himalayas with long, slim grains. More expensive than other long-grained rice but considered to be the best.

Baste — to moisten meat, poultry or fish by spooning over juices from the dish while cooking.

Caramelise — obtain a brown syrupy mixture by boiling sugar in a liquid.

Dice — to cut into small cubes.

Escallop — a very thin slice of meat. Usually applies to veal although turkey escallops are now available.

Fold — a gentle stirring action to combine a whisked or creamed mixture with other ingredients so that it retains its lightness.

Fromage Frais — a soft cheese produced by introducing an acid-making culture to warm pasteurised skimmed milk which causes the milk to curdle. The curd is separated from the whey to produce the finished cheese. Many fruit-flavoured varieties of this popular cheese are now available.

Garam Masala — a combination of pungent ground mixed spices used in Indian cookery. Ready-mixed versions are available from large supermarkets and delicatessens.

Garnish — an edible savoury decoration such as parsley.

Kebab — cubes of marinaded meat, poultry or fish grilled on a skewer.

Liquor — the liquid in which meat, fish or vegetables is cooked.

Mange-tout — tiny peas in the pod which are eaten whole. Sometimes known as sugar peas.

Marinade — a blend of seasonings and spices and liquid such as wine, oil and vinegar which is used to soak meat prior to cooking.

Medallions — small rounds of meat.

Melba Toast — thin crisp slices of toasted bread. Also available in packets from the dry biscuit section of supermarkets.

Parboil — boiling vegetables until they are partly cooked then finished off by some other method.

Poach — cooking gently in an open pan of simmering liquid. Usually applied to fish and eggs.

Reduce — the process of boiling a liquid in an uncovered pan in order to evaporate surplus liquid and give a more syrupy result.

Sauté — to fry gently in a little fat or oil.

Scant — just under the stated measurement.

Score — making shallow cuts on the surface of food.

Simmer — keeping a liquid at just below boiling point.

Soured Cream — made from fresh cream which has been commercially treated, rather like yoghurt, to give it a special flavour and texture. Soured cream is not as rich as ordinary cream and is ideal for both savoury and sweet dishes.

Vinaigrette Dressing — a mixture of one part vinegar to two parts oil and sometimes flavoured with herbs and spices.

Vol-au-Vent — a round or oval case made of puff pastry and filled with a sweet or savoury mixture. Ready-made frozen vol-au-vents are available at larger supermarkets.

Yeast Extract — a concentrated flavouring for savoury dishes. In the vegetarian diet it replaces meat stock cubes. Marmite is probably the best known brand but others are widely available.

5 VEGETABLES, CHEESE AND EGGS

Although these recipes are not aimed totally at the vegetarian, there are several in this chapter, and throughout the book, which satisfy this criterion. (See also chapters on Pasta, Grains and Pulses and Television Suppers, Snacks and Salads.)

However, whether for health, social or economical reasons, statistics show that more people are eating less meat. This section is largely aimed at those who perhaps like to include a couple of meatless, or almost meatless, meals in their weekly menu.

Soya bean products, like tofu which is available in varying textures, make a good alternative to meat and fish. Rich in protein, minerals and vitamins, tofu is both healthier and cheaper. It can be shallow and deep fried and marinaded and makes an ideal substitute for meat in many of the recipes in the book.

Soya mince is also available and it is well worth keeping a couple of packets in store for a stock cupboard Bolognese sauce. (See chapter 6 on Pasta.)

CHEESE PLATE PIE   *Serves 4*

This is a shallow tin plate pie with a light and fluffy cheese filling. It is good hot or cold but is best eaten on the day of cooking. Serve with buttered new potatoes and salad.

Preparation time: 10 mins.   Cooking time: 20 mins.

2 oz (50g) butter or margarine
4 oz (100g) mature Cheddar cheese, grated
2 eggs, beaten
Salt and pepper
1 lb (450g) short crust frozen pastry, defrosted

1. Pre-heat oven to 220°C (425°F) or Gas No 7.

2. Melt butter or margarine in a small saucepan, then stir in the grated cheese, beaten egg and seasoning.

3. Heat gently, stirring all the time, for about 5 minutes, until mixture thickens and coats the back of the spoon. Set aside to cool.

4. Meanwhile roll out half the pastry and line an 8 to 9" (20 to 23cm) tin pie plate. Trim edges.

5. Spread on the cheese mixture to within ½" (1.5cm) of the edge. Brush edges with beaten egg or milk.

6. Roll out remaining pastry and cover pie. Trim and pinch edges, brush the top with beaten egg or milk and bake for about 15 minutes until well risen and golden.

BAKED TOMATOES WITH HERB AND CRUMB TOPPING   *Serves 4*

This is a convenient way of using up an autumn glut of tomatoes, or when shop prices are low. Serve with cold meat or a mixed bean salad and crusty rolls.

Preparation time: 6 mins.   *Cooking time: 15 mins.*

12 average sized tomatoes
Salt and pepper
1 teasp sugar
3 oz (75g) parsley and thyme stuffing mix
2 tablsp cooking oil

1. Pre-heat oven to 190°C (375°F) or Gas No 5.

2. Cut each tomato into three thick slices and arrange in an ovenproof dish.

3. Season with salt and pepper and sprinkle on the sugar.

4. Shake the dry stuffing mix evenly over the tomatoes and trickle over the oil.

5. Cook in oven for about 15 minutes until the topping is golden.

VEGETABLE CURRY   *Serves 4*

At first glance this recipe has a rather off-putting long list of ingredients, but it is a throw-it-all-in-the-pot meal and quite quick to prepare. Serve with pillau rice or naan bread.

Preparation time: 15 mins.   *Cooking time: 40 mins.*

1 teasp coriander seeds
2 teasp cumin
1 teasp garam masala
1 teasp mustard seeds
2 cloves garlic, peeled and finely chopped
6 tablsp cooking oil
1 large onion, peeled and chopped
2 fresh chillies, chopped OR 1 teasp crushed dried
    chillies
½ lb (225g) button mushrooms
1 aubergine, cut into dice

(continued overleaf)

(Vegetable Curry continued)

½ lb (225g) leeks, sliced
4 medium potatoes, peeled and cut into dice
1 cauliflower, broken into florets
14 oz (397g) can peeled tomatoes
1 teasp salt
Pepper

1. Pre-heat oven to 170°C (325°F) or Gas No 3.

2. Crush the coriander seeds with a rolling pin.

3. Sauté coriander, cumin, garam masala, mustard seeds and garlic in the oil for a couple of minutes.

4. Add all the remaining ingredients and sauté for about 10 minutes, stirring frequently.

5. Turn the mixture into an ovenproof casserole with lid and cook for about 30 minutes until the vegetables are tender. Adjust seasoning if necessary.

BACON AND EGG PIE   *Serves 4*

This is usually successful with children. It is just as good served hot with vegetables and potatoes as cold with salad.

Preparation time: 15 mins.   Cooking time: 20 mins.

6 oz (175g) smoked streaky bacon, diced
½ tablsp oil
3 eggs
3 tablsp milk
1 lb (450g) short crust frozen pastry, defrosted

1. Pre-heat oven to 220°C (425°F) or Gas No 7.

2. Fry the bacon in the oil for about 15 minutes until fairly crispy.

3. Beat the eggs and milk together.

4. Roll out half the pastry and line a 10 inch (26cm) shallow tin plate. Sprinkle the bacon over the pastry and pour on all but a tablespoon of the egg mixture.

5. Using the reserved egg, brush the edges of the pastry. Roll out the remaining pastry and use to cover the pie. Press down firmly, pinch edges and brush the top with the reserved egg.

6. Bake in oven for about 12 minutes, then turn down oven to 170°C (325°F) or Gas No 3 for a further 8 minutes until well risen and golden.

SPANISH OMELETTE   *Serves 4*

Omelettes are a favourite stand-by for an economical and quick meal. To make the dish more substantial you can add almost anything — grated cheese, fried mushrooms, prawns, chopped tomato, diced ham, spicy sausage and corn — or try a combination of several. A Spanish omelette is made differently from the others, more like a pancake. When it is cooked, serve cut in wedges with salad and fried matchstick potatoes. Omelettes are also good served with ratatouille (see page 32).

Preparation time: 8 mins. Cooking time: 25 mins.

1 onion, peeled and chopped
1 small potato, peeled and diced
1 courgette, sliced
1 tablsp cooking oil
2 tomatoes, chopped
6 eggs
2 tablsp water
Salt and pepper

1. Heat the grill.

2. Fry the onion, potato and courgette in the oil for about 15 minutes until tender.

3. Stir in the tomatoes.

4. Beat the eggs, water and seasoning together and pour into the vegetables. Cook for about 5 minutes until the eggs are brown and set on the underside.

5. Pop the frying pan under the grill and cook for a few minutes until the omelette is golden. Serve immediately.

OMELETTE AUX FINES HERBS   *Serves 1*

After a long, hard day there is nothing nicer, or quicker, than a light omelette with a golden outside, fluffy and creamy inside and flavoured with chopped fresh herbs from the garden.

Preparation time: 5 mins.   Cooking time: 5 mins.

2-3 eggs, depending on size
1 teasp water
Salt and pepper
1 tablsp roughly chopped herbs — chives, parsley,
**   tarragon and chervil**
Knob butter for frying

1. Beat the eggs, water, seasoning and herbs together, just enough to break down the egg.

2. Melt the butter in an omelette, or small frying pan, and when fairly hot pour in the egg mixture.

3. As the egg begins to set around the edges, use a spatula or spoon to draw the cooked egg into the centre, thus letting uncooked mixture run underneath.

4. When the egg has set, cook for a minute until golden underneath. Fold the omelette in half and serve immediately.

RATATOUILLE   *Serves 4*

This is a well-known, classic vegetable dish and has a flavour like no other. The Mediterranean aroma of garlic frying in olive oil is delicious in itself! Serve with hot garlic bread.

Preparation time: 12 mins.   Cooking time: 30 mins.

4 tablsp olive oil
2 onions, peeled and sliced
1 aubergine, diced
4 courgettes, sliced
4 tomatoes, cut into pieces
1 green pepper, de-seeded and sliced
1 red pepper, de-seeded and sliced
2 cloves garlic, peeled and finely chopped
2 tablsp tomato purée
Salt and pepper

1. Heat the oil in a large saucepan.

2. Add all the prepared vegetables, tomato purée and seasoning.

3. Stir over a low heat for 5 minutes, then put a lid on the saucepan and cook for a further 25 minutes. The vegetables should be soft and well blended but not pulpy.

EGGS DUCHESSE   *Serves 4*

A rather grand name for glorified scrambled eggs! It is particularly good served on squares of crispy fried bread — naughty but nice! (For a single serving use 2 eggs, 1 tablespoon of milk, 1 tablespoon of dried mushrooms, 1 slice of ham and a knob of butter the size of a hazelnut.)

Preparation time: 15 mins.   Cooking time: 10 mins.

Handful dried sliced mushrooms
6 eggs
3 tablsp milk
Salt and pepper
4 oz (100g) cooked ham, diced
Large knob butter

1. Put the mushrooms in a cup and pour on boiling water. Leave for 15 minutes then drain.

2. Beat the eggs, milk and seasoning together and add the diced ham and drained mushrooms.

3. Melt the butter in a small saucepan, pour in the egg mixture and cook gently like scrambled eggs, stirring continuously.

MUSHROOM AND BROCCOLI PIE   *Serves 4*

Mushrooms, onion and broccoli combine with a thick gravy, flavoured with yeast extract and tomato purée, to make a tasty pie. Lightly cooked carrot sticks make a perfect accompaniment.

Preparation time: 10 mins.   Cooking time: 20 mins.

1 tablsp butter or margarine
8 oz (225g) mushrooms, sliced
1 onion, peeled and chopped
8 oz (225g) broccoli
¼ pt (150ml) water
1 tablsp flour
1 tablsp tomato purée
2 teasp yeast extract
8 oz (225g) frozen short crust pastry, defrosted

1. Pre-heat oven to 220°C (425°F) or Gas No 7.

2. Melt the butter or margarine in a frying pan and sauté the mushrooms and onion for about 10 minutes until tender.

3. Meanwhile cut the broccoli into small florets and slice the stalks. Bring the ¼ pt (150ml) water to the boil, add the broccoli and simmer for five minutes. Drain and reserve the liquor.

4. Stir in the flour, tomato purée, yeast extract and broccoli water into the mixture in the frying pan. Stir over a low heat until thickened.

5. Add the broccoli and pour the mixture into an oval or circular pie dish.

6. Roll out the pastry and cover. If liked, brush with beaten egg or milk then bake for about 10 minutes until golden.

SPINACH CANNELLONI   *Serves 4*

If you can prepare this dish the evening before eating, the cannelloni will have softened and therefore only about 10 minutes' cooking time is needed.

Preparation time: 10 mins.   Cooking time: 10-40 mins.

1 lb (450g) frozen spinach, defrosted and drained
2 tablsp shelled whole hazelnuts
Salt and pepper
10 cannelloni
14 oz (397g) can chopped chilli tomatoes
7 oz (200g) feta cheese

1. Pre-heat the oven to 180°C (350°F) or Gas No 4.

2. Mix the spinach, nuts and seasoning together in a bowl and use the mixture to stuff the cannelloni.

3. Lay the cannelloni close together in a shallow ovenproof dish.

4. Pour over the tomatoes, together with a splash of boiling water.

5. Crumble the feta cheese over the top and bake for about 40 minutes. (If the dish is prepared beforehand, the cannelloni will soften and need less cooking time, as stated at the start of the recipe.)

VEGETABLE HOT POT WITH HERB DUMPLINGS   *Serves 4*

The vegetables listed in this recipe are a suggestion — any

combination can be used. Aim for about 2½-3 lb (1.1 - 1.4kg) vegetables (unprepared weight). The addition of baked beans enhances the flavour and tempts children to eat vegetables! The dumpling mix contains suet but vegetarians could substitute small balls of cheese scone mixture.

Preparation time: 12 mins.   Cooking time: 50 mins.

2 teasp yeast extract
½ pt (300ml) boiling water
Cauliflower, broken into florets
Onion, peeled and roughly chopped
Parsnip, peeled and diced
Carrot, peeled and sliced
Leeks, sliced
Celery, sliced
Potatoes, peeled and diced
Green pepper, de-seeded and sliced
Salt and pepper
16 oz (450g) can baked beans
8 oz (225g) suet dumpling mix
2 teasp mixed dried herbs

1. Pre-heat oven to 190°C (375°F) or Gas No 5.

2. Put the yeast extract into a large casserole and pour on the boiling water.

3. Add all the prepared vegetables, seasoning and baked beans. Cover and cook in oven for 35 minutes.

4. Meanwhile stir the dumpling mix and herbs together in a bowl and make up with water according to manufacturer's instructions. Form into eight small balls.

5. Drop the dumplings into the casserole and cook for a further 15 minutes.

AUBERGINE BAKE
Serves 4

A truly delicious dish as the cream and stock combine to complement the creamy texture of the vegetables. Serve with garlic bread.

Preparation time: 10 mins.   Cooking time: 40 mins.

2 onions, peeled and sliced
1 large aubergine, sliced thinly
8 oz (225g) mushrooms, sliced
Salt and pepper
1 tablsp flour
1 stock cube, made up with ¼ pt (150ml) water
5 fl oz (150ml) single cream
3 tablsp white wine OR water
3 oz (75g) commercially prepared brown breadcrumbs

1. Pre-heat oven to 190°C (375°F) or Gas No 5.

2. Layer half the onions, aubergine and mushrooms in a large ovenproof casserole.

3. Season well and sprinkle the flour over the vegetables. Layer the remaining vegetables on top, finishing with the aubergine.

4. Pour on the stock, cream and wine or water.

5. Sprinkle the breadcrumbs over and bake for about 40 minutes.

VEGETABLE INDIENNE
Serves 4

Subtly flavoured with a hint of lemon and ginger, these tooth-tender vegetables make a wonderful healthy supper dish. Vegetarians can omit the prawns and substitute bean sprouts and a few chestnuts. Serve with hot garlic bread.

Preparation time: 12 mins.   Cooking time: 25 mins.

4 tablsp cooking oil
1 onion, peeled and sliced
Large knob ginger, peeled and grated
12 oz (350g) broccoli, cut into small pieces
1 lb (450g) courgettes, sliced
1 red pepper, de-seeded and sliced
1 yellow pepper, de-seeded and sliced
8 oz (225g) mange-tout
2 teasp curry paste
Juice 1 lemon
1 teasp yeast extract, mixed with ¼ pt (150ml) water
8 oz (225g) peeled prawns

1. Heat the oil in a wok or very large frying pan; failing these
    a large saucepan will do.

2. Add the onion, ginger, broccoli, courgettes, peppers and
    mange-tout.

3. Stir fry the vegetables for 15 minutes.

4. Stir in the curry paste, lemon juice, yeast extract and water.
    Cook gently for a further 10 minutes.

5. Add the prawns and serve garnished with chopped fresh
    coriander if liked.

MUSHROOM AND ASPARAGUS
VOL-AU-VENTS   *Serves 4*

Frozen ready-prepared vol-au-vents, which are made with puff
pastry, are a great help to the after work cook. They come in three
sizes — cocktail, medium and king-size. All manner of fillings
can be devised to make a quick supper dish. (See also chapters
on Fish, Meat, Television Suppers and Desserts.) Experiment with
your own particular favourite combinations.

Preparation time: 8 mins.   Cooking time: 17 mins.

4 king-size frozen vol-au-vents
4 oz (100g) mushrooms, sliced
1 clove garlic, peeled and chopped
1 tablsp cooking oil
10.4 oz (295g) can condensed mushroom soup
Small can (12 oz/340g) cut asparagus or tips, drained
Ground black pepper

1. Pre-heat oven to 220°C (425°F) or Gas No 7. Cook the vol-au-vents in the oven for about 12 minutes until well risen and lightly brown.

2. Meanwhile fry the mushrooms and garlic in the oil for about 10 minutes until tender.

3. Put the soup in a bowl and mix in the drained mushrooms, garlic, asparagus and a good grind of black pepper.

4. Remove lids from the vol-au-vents and pull out uncooked pastry and discard.

5. Fill the vol-au-vents with the mushroom mixture — pop on the lids and heat in the oven for 5 minutes. Serve with new potatoes and salad.

HALLOUMI PAN FRY   *Serves 4*

This quick recipe is a type of omelette from Cyprus which was given to me by George, who is now living in the U.K. Halloumi is Cypriot cheese made with sheep's milk, which rather resembles Mozarella in flavour and texture though not as stringy. It is available from specialist shops but you could substitute other cheese. Serve with tomato salad and sesame seed bread.

Preparation time: 5 mins.   Cooking time: 15 mins.

1 small onion, peeled and chopped
2 tablsp olive oil

(continued overleaf)

(Halloumi Pan Fry continued)

4 oz (100g) Halloumi cheese, sliced
Small bunch flat leaf parsley, roughly chopped
Few black olives, stoned
6 eggs
Salt and pepper
1 tablsp water

1. Fry the onion in the oil for about 10 minutes until tender.

2. Push the onion to one side and add the cheese, frying for a few minutes until each side is brown.

3. Add the parsley and olives, stirring over a low heat for a couple of minutes to mix the ingredients.

4. Beat the eggs, seasoning and water together and pour into the pan.

5. As the egg cooks around the sides, draw it into the centre letting the uncooked egg run underneath. When the mixture has set like an omelette, cut into four wedges and serve.

CHESTNUT DHANSAK   *Serves 4*

Of Indian origin, this deliciously flavoured recipe traditionally uses lamb and lentils. Here the 'meat' is whole chestnuts, making it ideal for vegetarians. If you can get to a delicatessen, the cooked dry, or vacuum-packed, chestnuts are the closest in flavour and texture to the fresh nut. Canned whole chestnuts are available from large supermarkets.

Preparation time: 10 mins.   Cooking time: 25 mins.

5 tablsp cooking oil
2 teasp coriander seeds, crushed
½ teasp chilli powder
1 teasp turmeric

1 teasp cumin
1 aubergine, cut into chunks
1 onion, peeled and chopped
4 oz (100g) red lentils
14 oz (397g) can chopped tomatoes
15 oz (425g) whole chestnuts, drained but reserve liquor if canned
12 oz (350g) spinach, washed and sliced
Salt and pepper
5 fl oz (150ml) carton natural yoghurt
Fresh coriander for garnish (optional)

1. Heat the oil in a large saucepan and add the next six ingredients.

2. Fry gently for 5 minutes, stirring well, then add the lentils, tomatoes, chestnuts and the liquor made up to ¼ pt (150ml) with water.

3. Pile the spinach on top with a generous shake of salt and pepper. Bring to the boil, put on a lid and simmer gently for 20 minutes, stirring occasionally.

4. Stir in the yoghurt and serve garnished with chopped coriander if liked.

Serve accompanied with brown rice or naan bread.

VEGETABLE AND CHEESE BAKE   *Serves 4*

A mixture of grated cheese and potato gives a tasty crunchy topping to vegetables in onion sauce. Use any combination of cooked vegetables but if none are to hand, a large packet of frozen broccoli, cauliflower and baby carrots gives excellent results.

Preparation time: 12 mins.   Cooking time: 30 mins.

2 packets (standard/25g size) onion sauce mix (make ½
   pint each)
2 teasp mustard powder (optional)
1 pt (500ml) milk
Freshly ground black pepper
2 lb (907g) cooked mixed vegetables or frozen pack
2 large potatoes, peeled and coarsely grated
4 oz (100g) mature Cheddar cheese, grated

1. Pre-heat oven to 180°C (350°F) or Gas No 4.

2. Empty the sauce mixes into a saucepan and add the mustard
    powder if using.

3. Make the sauce according to manufacturer's instructions with
    the milk. Season with pepper.

4. Stir the vegetables into the sauce and pour into an ovenproof
    dish.

5. Mix the potatoes and cheese together and arrange on top of
    the vegetables.

6. Bake for 30 minutes until the topping is brown and crispy.

Tip: A variation on the previous recipe can be made by mixing
cooked vegetables with a cheese sauce, but instead of the potato
and cheese topping, split 4 croissants horizontally and use as a top
and bottom 'pie crust'.

6 PASTA, GRAINS AND PULSES

PASTA

The number of quick and tasty sauces which can be made to create interesting pasta dishes is limited only by your imagination. All the following recipes can be prepared and cooked in less time than it takes to down a gin and tonic after a hard day's work! You'd pay a fortune for such a meal at an Italian restaurant!

Dried pasta, sold in packets, is the most commonly used. However many people consider fresh pasta superior in flavour, and although more expensive, it is now available from large supermarkets and speciality shops.

Depending on appetite, allow between 2-3 oz (50-75g) of pasta per person. Dried varieties take about 8-10 minutes to cook, fresh takes less time. Cook in boiling salted water to which a little oil has been added. This prevents the pasta clogging together when cooked.

CREAMY NOODLES   *Serves 4*

Preparation time: 10 mins.   Cooking time: 10 mins.

8-12 oz (225-350g) noodles
Knob butter or margarine
6 oz (175g) mushrooms, sliced
6 oz (175g) ham, cut in strips
5 fl oz (150ml) double cream
2 oz (50g) mature Cheddar cheese, grated
1 tablsp milk

1. Cook the noodles in boiling salted water for about 8 minutes until tender.

2. Meanwhile, melt the butter or margarine in a frying pan and sauté the mushrooms for a few minutes until tender.

3. Add the ham, cream, cheese and milk and stir over a low heat until the cheese has melted.

4. Drain the noodles and toss through the sauce.

5. Serve sprinkled with chopped parsley if liked.

LEMON AND WALNUT TAGLIATELLE   *Serves 4*

This is a wonderfully healthy and fresh-looking pasta dish with crunchy nuts and courgettes in a tangy lemon cream sauce.

Preparation time: 12 mins. Cooking time: 15 mins.

4 courgettes, cut into small dice
Grated rind and juice of 2 lemons
½ tablsp cooking oil
Knob butter or margarine
8-12 oz (225-350g) tagliatelle
Salt and pepper
2 tablsp walnut pieces
½ pt (300ml) single cream

1. Fry the courgettes and grated lemon rind in the oil and butter, or margarine, for about 10 minutes until tender.

2. Meanwhile cook the tagliatelle in boiling salted water for about 8 minutes.

3. Add seasoning, lemon juice and walnuts to the courgettes and when simmering, stir in the cream.

4. Drain the tagliatelle and fold through the sauce.

5. Garnish with chopped parsley if liked.

TAGLIATELLE IN SPICY TOMATO SAUCE
Serves 4

This mildly spiced sauce is delicious with pasta and is so quick and simple to make. (See page 23, for serving one or two.)

Preparation time: 5 mins.   Cooking time: 12 mins.

1 onion, peeled and chopped
1 tablsp cooking oil
8-12 oz (225-350g) tagliatelle
4 oz (100g) thinly sliced peppered salami
14 oz (397g) can chopped chilli tomatoes
Grated Parmesan cheese for garnish

1. Sauté the onion in the oil for about 10 minutes until soft.

2. Meanwhile cook the tagliatelle in boiling salted water for about 8 minutes until tender.

3. Cut the slices of salami into quarters and add to the onion. Fry gently for a couple of minutes.

4. Stir in the chopped tomatoes and simmer for a further two minutes.

5. Drain the tagliatelle and fold through the sauce. Serve sprinkled with Parmesan cheese.

SPAGHETTI PROVENÇAL   *Serves 4*

This is a nice rich vegetable sauce to serve with spaghetti. Hot garlic bread makes a good accompaniment. (For a single serving use 1 small onion, 1 courgette, omit the leeks, 1 oz (25g) mushrooms, half a tablespoon of oil, 2-3 oz (50-75g) spaghetti, and substitute the can of tomatoes for 2 chopped fresh tomatoes, a squeeze of tomato purée and a dash of water. Or see page 23.)

Preparation time: 10 mins.   Cooking time: 15 mins.

1 onion, peeled and chopped
3 courgettes, sliced
2 leeks, sliced
4 oz (100g) mushrooms, sliced
2 tablsp cooking oil
8-12 oz (225-350g) spaghetti
14 oz (397g) can tomatoes
1 tablsp chopped fresh oregano or 1 teasp dried
Salt and freshly ground black pepper

1. Fry the onion, courgettes, leeks and mushrooms gently in the oil for about 15 minutes.

2. Meanwhile cook the spaghetti in boiling salted water for about 8 minutes.

3. Stir the tomatoes, herbs and seasoning into the vegetable mixture and cook for a couple of minutes.

4. Drain the spaghetti and fold through the sauce.

SPAGHETTI VERDE   *Serves 4*

This is simple and delicious but it is essential to use fresh herbs. Serve with a mixed salad.

Preparation time: 8 mins.   Cooking time: 8 mins.

2 cloves garlic, peeled and finely chopped
Small knob butter or margarine
8-12 oz (225-350g) spaghetti
Juice 1 lemon
2 tablsp chopped parsley
1 teasp each chopped rosemary, chives, chervil, basil and
    oregano
Butter
Freshly ground black pepper

1. Fry the garlic in the butter or margarine until tender.

2. Meanwhile cook the spaghetti in boiling salted water for about
    8 minutes.

3. Add the lemon juice, parsley and herbs to the garlic and cook
    for a couple of minutes.

4. Drain the spaghetti and fold through the herb mixture, adding
    an extra knob of butter and some freshly ground black pepper.

PASTA NIÇOISE   *Serves 4*

There is a large selection of pasta shapes available, from bows,
spirals and tubes to shells, wheels and alphabet letters. (See page
23, for serving one or two.)

Preparation time: 5 mins.   Cooking time: 15 mins.

1 clove garlic, peeled and finely chopped
1 onion, peeled and chopped
½ tablsp cooking oil
14 oz (397g) can chopped tomatoes
Salt and pepper
8-12 oz (225-350g) pasta shapes
7 oz (198g) can tuna fish in oil, drained

1. Fry the garlic and onion in the oil for a couple of minutes.

2. Stir in the tomatoes and seasoning and simmer for about 15 minutes until mixture has reduced slightly.

3. Meanwhile cook the pasta shapes in boiling salted water for about 8 minutes or until tender.

4. Stir the drained tuna fish into the tomato mixture and cook for a couple of minutes.

5. Drain the pasta and fold through the sauce. If liked, sprinkle with grated cheese.

TAGLIATELLE WITH SPICY AUBERGINE

Serves 4

Anyone who loves aubergine and the subtle spices of Indian food will adore this pasta sauce.

Preparation time: 10 mins.   Cooking time: 15 mins.

1 aubergine, cut into small dice
1 onion, peeled and chopped
½ teasp cayenne
1 teasp turmeric
1 teasp fenugreek seeds
Salt and pepper
4 tablsp cooking oil
8-12 oz (225-350g) tagliatelle
1 tablsp chopped fresh coriander
5 fl oz (150ml) carton soured cream

1. Fry the aubergine, onion, cayenne, turmeric, fenugreek seeds, salt and pepper in the oil for about 12 minutes until tender. Stir frequently during cooking.

2. Meanwhile cook the tagliatelle in boiling salted water for about 8 minutes.

3. Stir the coriander and soured cream into the aubergine mixture and heat for a couple of minutes.

4.   Drain the tagliatelle and fold through the sauce.

CRUNCHY PEANUT AND CELERY
PASTA
Serves 4

This sauce tends to be a favourite with children, probably because of the creamy peanut flavour.

Preparation time: 10 mins.   Cooking time: 20 mins.

3 sticks celery, sliced thinly
4 oz (100g) button mushrooms, sliced
1 tablsp cooking oil
2 tablsp crunchy peanut butter
1 tablsp tomato purée
½ stock cube made up with ¼ pt (150ml) water
8-12 oz (225-350g) tagliatelle or other pasta
2 tablsp soured cream

1.   Sauté the celery and mushrooms for 5 minutes in the oil.

2.   Stir in peanut butter, tomato purée and stock. Simmer without a lid, stirring occasionally, for about 15 minutes until the liquid has reduced and thickened.

3.   Meanwhile cook the pasta in boiling salted water for about 8 minutes.

4.   Stir in the soured cream to the celery and mushroom mixture.

5.   Drain the pasta and fold through the sauce.

BROCCOLI AND ROQUEFORT CREAM *Serves 4*

This is a rich cream sauce highly flavoured with blue cheese, which goes well with a bland food such as pasta. Tiny florets of broccoli add colour and a crunchy texture.

Preparation time: 10 mins.   Cooking time: 10 mins.

8-12 oz (225-350g) tagliatelle
½ lb (225g) broccoli, cut into small florets
¼ pt (150ml) double cream
4 oz (100g) Roquefort, or other blue veined cheese
2 tablsp Greek yoghurt
Freshly ground black pepper

1. Cook the tagliatelle in boiling salted water for about 8 minutes.

2. Cook the broccoli in a little salted water for 3-4 minutes until just tender. Drain.

3. Put the cream in a small saucepan and crumble in the cheese. Heat gently until the cheese has melted.

4. Stir in the yoghurt, black pepper and broccoli.

5. Drain the tagliatelle and fold through the sauce.

STORE CUPBOARD SPAGHETTI BOLOGNESE
Serves 4

If shopping for fresh produce has been impossible, these store-cupboard ingredients make a tasty and filling meal which is also suitable for vegetarians. There is hardly any preparation necessary so the recipe is ideal for a late night impromptu supper. Soya products are available from health food shops and some supermarkets. (See page 23, for serving one or two.)

Preparation time: 3 mins. Cooking time: 15 mins.

8 oz (225g) packet minced soya protein
14 oz (397g) can chopped tomatoes
Handful dried onion OR 1 peeled and chopped onion
Handful dried sliced mushrooms
Packet (standard/40g size) Bolognese sauce mix
    (makes ½ pint)
½ pt (300ml) water
8-12 oz (225-350g) spaghetti
Few black olives, stoned (optional)
Grated Parmesan cheese

1. Put the soya mince, tomatoes, onion, mushrooms and sauce mix in a saucepan.

2. Stir in the water, bring to the boil and simmer gently for 15 minutes.

3. Meanwhile cook the spaghetti in boiling salted water until tender, about 12 minutes. Drain.

4. If using olives, stir them into the Bolognese mixture.

5. Arrange the spaghetti on plates, pile the Bolognese mixture in the centre and serve with Parmesan cheese.

SALMON PARISIENNE   *Serves 4*

A quick fork supper made with canned salmon, pasta and vegetables in a creamy wine and herb sauce. Serve with garlic bread.

Preparation time: 8 mins.   Cooking time: 10 mins.

6 oz (175g) thin cut macaroni or other pasta shapes
1 red pepper, de-seeded and chopped
4 oz (100g) fresh or frozen green beans
Packet (standard/17g size) white sauce mix (makes ½ pint)
¼ pt (150ml) white wine ⎫
¼ pt (150ml) milk ⎬ **or ½ pt (300ml milk)**
14 oz/400g can flageolet beans
15½ oz/440g can salmon, drained and flaked
2 tablsp single cream (optional)
1 teasp chopped fresh dill (optional)
Salt and pepper

1. Cook the macaroni in boiling salted water for about 8 minutes until tender. Drain.

2. Cook the pepper and green beans in a little salted water for about 8 minutes until just tender.

3.   Meanwhile make up the sauce mix with the wine and milk, according to manufacturer's instructions.

4.   Add the flageolet beans, salmon, drained pasta, pepper and green beans, mixing together gently but thoroughly.

5.   Stir in the cream and dill if using and season to taste.

BEEF CHOW MEIN   *Serves 4*

A very quick Anglicised — but tasty — version!

Preparation time: 10 mins.   Cooking time: 15 mins.

8 oz (225g) Chinese noodles or vermicelli
1 tablsp cooking oil
Juice 1 lemon
1 tablsp soy sauce
2 teasp paprika
1 onion, peeled and chopped
2 cloves garlic, peeled and crushed
4 oz (100g) mushrooms, sliced
Handful frozen peas
7 oz (200g) can sweetcorn, drained
Small (8 oz/230g) can water chestnuts, sliced
12 oz (350g) rump steak, sliced thinly

1.   Cook the noodles or vermicelli in boiling salted water until tender, about 8 minutes.

2.   Meanwhile heat the oil, lemon juice, soy sauce and paprika in a large frying pan.

3.   Add the onion, garlic, mushrooms, peas, sweetcorn and water chestnuts and cook gently for 8 minutes.

4.   Add the steak and cook quickly for about 5 minutes, stirring all the time.

5.   Fold the drained pasta through the meat mixture before serving.

GRAINS

Unless you are a strict vegetarian, the most common grain used by the average cook is rice. Others are wheat, corn, barley, millet, oats and rye. Grains provide valuable fibre, some minerals and have a low fat content.

Brown rice is now preferred by many for its nutty flavour and firm texture, compared to the softer, blander taste of white rice. Wild rice, although expensive, is also popular. It is not strictly a rice, being the grains from wild grasses, but is delicious and well worth keeping in stock.

Traditionally a risotto should be creamier than a pillau. Unless you use the special Italian risotto rice, which is sold at some supermarkets, you are unlikely to achieve any difference.

You can use just about anything in a risotto or pillau. Experiment with your own favourite combinations of meat, fish, vegetables and even fruit. Some of the following recipes include brown rice, but by substituting white rice the cooking time is halved: 30-40 minutes for brown and 10-20 minutes for white. Allow between 2-3 oz (50-75g) of rice per person.

LAMB PILAU *Serves 4*

Lamb and coriander complement each other beautifully, resulting in a succulent and tasty supper dish.

Preparation time: 10 mins.   Cooking time: 40 mins.

2 tablsp cooking oil
1 onion, peeled and chopped
1 teasp coriander seeds
½ lb (225g) button mushrooms
12 oz (350g) leg or fillet lamb
Salt and pepper
2 tablsp sultanas
12 oz (350g) brown rice (for white rice, see above)
1 stock cube, made up with 1¼ pt (650ml) water

1.   Heat the oil in a large saucepan and add the onion.

2. Crush the coriander seeds with a rolling pin and add them to the pan together with the mushrooms.

3. Cut the lamb into bite-size pieces and add to the pan together with seasoning, sultanas and rice.

4. Fry for about 5 minutes to brown the meat.

5. Stir in the stock, bring to the boil and simmer with a lid on for about 40 minutes. Check during the last ten minutes and add more water if necessary.

PORK RISOTTO WITH CIDER   *Serves 4*

For economy, reduce the amount of meat and add more vegetables.

Preparation time: 10 mins.   Cooking time: 40 mins.

1 lb (450g) leg of pork or tenderloin
1 onion, peeled and chopped
1 cooking apple, peeled, cored and sliced
2 sticks celery, sliced
8 oz (225g) brown rice (for white rice, see page 53)
2 tablsp cooking oil
1 tablsp chopped fresh sage OR 1 teasp dried
2 teasp mustard powder
¾ pt (400ml) medium-sweet cider
1 stock cube, made up with ¼ pt (150ml) water
3 oz (75g) packet nuts and raisins
Salt and Pepper

1. Cut the pork into bite-size pieces and put it in a large saucepan together with the onion, apple, celery, rice and oil.

2. Fry over a high heat until the meat has browned on all sides.

3. Stir in all the remaining ingredients, bring to the boil and simmer gently for about 40 minutes with a lid on. Check during the last ten minutes and add a little water if necessary.

CHINESE EGG FRIED RICE   *Serves 4*

Serve on its own or with a tomato and cheese salad.

Preparation time: 10 mins.   Cooking time: 20 mins.

12 oz (350g) white long-grain rice
Salt
2 tablsp cooking oil
2 cloves garlic, peeled and finely chopped
4 spring onions, sliced
1 tablsp sesame seeds
1 red pepper, de-seeded and chopped
4 oz (100g) mushrooms, sliced
1 tablsp soy sauce
6 oz (175g) peeled prawns
Freshly ground black pepper
2 eggs, beaten

1. Cook the rice in boiling salted water until tender, about 10
    minutes. Drain.

2. Heat the oil in a large frying pan and add the garlic, spring
    onions, sesame seeds, red pepper and mushrooms. Fry until
    the vegetables are tender, about 10 minutes.

3. Stir in the drained rice, soy sauce, prawns and black pepper
    and fry for a further few minutes, stirring well.

4. Make a well in the centre of the rice and pour in the beaten
    egg. Fry over a high heat, stirring the egg well through the
    rice as it scrambles.

VEGETABLE RISOTTO   *Serves 4*

This mildly spiced risotto is ideal to serve with cold meat or
kebabs. On its own as a vegetarian meal it could be accompanied
by garlic bread or a cheese and tomato salad.

Preparation time: 12 mins.   Cooking time: 40 mins.

4 tablsp cooking oil
1 onion, peeled and chopped
2 leeks, washed and sliced
3 sticks celery, sliced
1 red pepper, de-seeded and sliced
4 oz (100g) mushrooms, sliced
Knob fresh ginger, grated
1 teasp garam masala
1 teasp turmeric
1 teasp chilli powder
2 teasp paprika
3 teasp yeast extract
8 oz (225g) brown rice (for white rice, see page 53)
Scant 1 pt (500ml) water
14 oz (397g) can chopped tomatoes

1. Heat the oil in a large saucepan and throw in all the prepared
   vegetables, ginger, spices, yeast extract and rice.

2. Fry for a few minutes stirring well.

3. Pour in the water, bring to boil and simmer, with the lid on,
   for about 40 minutes until the rice is tender. Check during the
   last ten minutes and add a little water if necessary.

4. Stir in the tomatoes and adjust seasoning.

AUBERGINE AND BULGAR WHEAT SUPPER

Serves 4

Serve with a green salad and fresh crusty bread.

Preparation time: 10 mins.   Cooking time: 15 mins.

3 oz (75g) bulgar wheat
2 aubergines, diced
2 onions, peeled and roughly chopped
3 fl oz (75ml) cooking oil

14 oz (397g) can tomatoes, drained
Dark and Spicy Dressing (see next recipe)
Salt and pepper
Chopped parsley for garnish (optional)

1. Put the bulgar wheat in a bowl and pour on enough boiling
    water to cover. Leave to stand for 15 minutes then drain.

2. Meanwhile fry the aubergines and onions in the oil until
    tender, about 15 minutes.

3. Stir in the tomatoes, bulgar wheat and about 4 tablespoons
    Dark and Spicy Dressing. Season and garnish with chopped
    parsley if liked.

DARK AND SPICY DRESSING

A piquant flavour which makes a good dressing for bland foods
such as bean salads.

5 fl oz (150ml) olive oil
2½ fl oz (75ml) raspberry vinegar OR red wine vinegar
Salt and pepper
½ teasp coriander
½ teasp cumin
Pinch cayenne
½ teasp mustard powder

Shake all the ingredients well together in a screw-top jar.

TUNA MEXICANA   *Serves 4*

This quick one-pan recipe makes a tasty supper dish and is similar
to the type of ready-prepared meal on the market, but infinitely
cheaper.

Preparation time: 8 mins.   Cooking time: 15 mins.

8 oz (225g) long-grain rice
1 onion, peeled and chopped
1 red pepper, de-seeded and sliced
2 tablsp tomato purée
2 teasp Mexican chilli seasoning
Salt and pepper
1 stock cube, made up with scant 1 pt (500ml) water
7 oz (200g) can sweetcorn, drained
8 oz (225g) can red kidney beans, drained
7 oz (200g) can tuna fish, drained and flaked
Juice 1 lemon

1. Put the rice, onion, red pepper, tomato purée, chilli seasoning, salt, pepper and stock into a saucepan.

2. Bring to the boil and simmer with a tight-fitting lid for about 15 minutes until the rice is tender.

3. Stir in the corn, beans, tuna fish and lemon juice and heat through for a couple of minutes. Serve with hot garlic bread.

BOMBAY PILAU   *Serves 4*

Another throw-it-all-in-the-pot recipe; everything except the fresh vegetables should be in stock! For added substance, meat-eaters could add some diced cooked ham, beef or chicken. The pilau is delicious served with Chick Pea Dhal (see next recipe).

Preparation time: 12 mins.   Cooking time: 20 mins.

4 tablsp cooking oil
2 teasp fenugreek seeds
2 teasp ground coriander
1 teasp ground cumin
1 teasp turmeric
½ teasp chilli powder
1 aubergine, diced
1 clove garlic, peeled and crushed
1 onion, peeled and chopped

4 oz (100g) mushrooms, sliced
Knob fresh ginger, peeled and coarsely grated
1 green pepper, de-seeded and diced
Salt and pepper
8 oz (225g) Basmati rice
15 fl oz (400ml) water

1. Heat the oil in a saucepan and add the next 5 ingredients.

2. Add the prepared vegetables to the spice mixture in the order given in the list of ingredients.

3. Add a generous shake of salt and pepper and cook gently for 10 minutes, stirring frequently.

4. Stir in the rice and cook for a couple of minutes.

5. Add the water, cover the pan and simmer for about 10 minutes until the rice is tender. (Check occasionally and add more water if the mixture is sticking.)

CHICK PEA DHAL

Serves 4

Preparation time: 5 mins.   Cooking time: 10 mins.

15½ oz (440g) can chick peas
Knob ginger, peeled and coarsely grated
1 fresh chilli, chopped
1 clove garlic, peeled and crushed
Juice 1 lemon
Salt and pepper
1 teasp mustard seeds
1 teasp turmeric
1 teasp ground cumin
1 teasp ground coriander

1. Put the chick peas, with the liquor, into a small saucepan and add all the other ingredients.

2. Bring to the boil then simmer for about 10 minutes until the liquid has reduced and thickened. Mash the chick peas a little with the back of a spoon.

Serve the Dhal as an accompaniment to other dishes.

PULSES

Pulse is the word which encompasses peas, beans and lentils. These rather humble, and much maligned objects, have enjoyed a renaissance in recent years. The range of canned and dried peas and beans sold by ordinary supermarkets has increased enormously.

Pulses are a rich source of protein and fibre and low in fat, but best of all perhaps, they are cheap.

Dried peas and beans have to be soaked overnight. This helps them to swell so that cooking time is reduced. Soaking also helps remove some of the agents which cause indigestion and flatulence. They also take about one hour to cook. For this reason I recommend using the excellent canned varieties on the market.

Lentils do not need soaking; split red lentils are the most common type and although quick to cook — about 15 minutes — they have a soft texture and go mushy.

Green or brown, also known as Continental, lentils, take longer to cook — about 45 minutes — but are preferred by many for their nutty flavour and ability to remain whole during cooking.

With the addition of flavourful herbs, spices and dressings, pulses can form the basis for all manner of interesting meals, both hot in casseroles or cold in salads.

LENTIL AND POTATO SUPPER   *Serves 4*

This makes a tasty and substantial supper dish and can be served with a green salad tossed in a well-flavoured dressing.

Preparation time: 10 mins.   *Cooking time: 30 mins.*

4 oz (100g) smoked streaky bacon, cut into pieces
2 celery sticks, sliced
1 onion, peeled and chopped
1 lb (450g) potatoes, peeled and diced
1 tablsp cooking oil
8 oz (225g) red lentils
14 oz (397g) can chopped tomatoes
1 tablsp Worcestershire sauce
1 stock cube, made up with 1 pt (500ml) water
Salt and pepper

1. Fry the bacon, celery, onion and potatoes in the oil for 10 minutes.

2. Stir in the lentils, tomatoes, Worcestershire sauce, stock and seasoning.

3. Bring to the boil and simmer gently for about 20 minutes until the lentils and vegetables are tender.

LENTIL MOUSSAKA   *Serves 4*

If liked, add some chopped salami or pepperoni at the same time as the tomatoes.

Preparation time: 10 mins.   Cooking time: 25 mins.

6 oz (175g) red lentils
1 onion, peeled and roughly chopped
Salt and pepper
2 tablsp yeast extract
1½ pt (800ml) water
1 aubergine, diced
4 tablsp cooking oil
1 egg, beaten
2 tablsp milk
3 oz (75g) mature Cheddar cheese, grated
2 oz (50g) hazelnuts
14 oz (397g) can chopped tomatoes

1. Pre-heat oven to 200°C (400°F) or Gas No 6.

2. Put the lentils, onion, seasoning, yeast extract and water in a saucepan. Bring to the boil and simmer for about 10 minutes until the lentils are tender.

3. Meanwhile fry the diced aubergine in the oil for about 10 minutes.

4. Mix the egg, milk and cheese together for the topping.

5. Drain the lentils, stir in the hazelnuts and tomatoes and pour the mixture into an ovenproof dish.

6. Top with the fried aubergine and pour on the cheese topping. Bake in oven for about 15 minutes.

CHEESE AND LENTIL LOAF   *Serves 4*

Cayenne pepper gives a kick to this supper dish. Add more or less according to personal taste. Serve hot or cold with a mayonnaise-based dressing such as mustard sauce (see page 86). Mixed salad and garlic bread make ideal accompaniments.

Preparation time: 10 mins.   Cooking time: 45 mins.

6 oz (175g) red lentils
1 teasp salt
12 fl oz (350ml) water
4 oz (100g) mature Cheddar cheese, grated
1 onion, peeled and chopped
½ teasp cayenne pepper
Juice ½ lemon
1 egg, beaten
3 tablsp single cream
Freshly ground black pepper

1. Pre-heat oven to 190°C (375°F) or Gas No 5.

2. Cook the lentils in the salt and water for about 15 minutes.

The mixture should resemble a stiff purée.

3. Stir in the grated cheese, onion, cayenne, lemon juice, egg, cream and pepper and mix thoroughly.

4. Pour the mixture into a greased loaf tin and bake for about 45 minutes. Leave to rest for 10 minutes before turning out.

CHICK PEA AND ARTICHOKE GRATIN *Serves 4*

Chick peas have a pleasant creamy texture and nutty flavour and blend well with artichokes in this crunchy topped supper dish.

Preparation time: 12 mins.   Cooking time: 12 mins.

14 oz (400g) can artichoke hearts
14 oz (400g) can chick peas
Packet (standard/25g size) onion sauce mix (makes ½ pint)
½ pint (300 ml) liquid (half vegetable juice, half milk)
3 oz (75g) packet parsley & thyme stuffing mix
2 oz (50g) mature Cheddar cheese, grated

1. Pre-heat oven to 200°C (400°F) or Gas No 6.

2. Drain the artichoke hearts, reserving the juice.

3. Drain the chick peas and mix both vegetables together in a bowl.

4. Make up the onion sauce according to manufacturer's instructions using half artichoke juice and half milk.

5. Mix the vegetables and sauce well together and turn mixture into a shallow ovenproof dish.

6. Combine the stuffing mix and cheese and sprinkle on top. Bake in oven for about 12 minutes.

BEAN AND VEGETABLE HOT POT   *Serves 4-6*

This is a chuck-it-all-in-a-recipe and resembles something between a casserole and a hearty soup. In spite of the use of Indian spices, the dish is not 'hot', or highly flavoured. You can use any combination of beans and vegetables, it will always taste good. Serve with crusty bread and butter.

Preparation time: 10 mins.   Cooking time: 20 mins.

2 medium potatoes, peeled and cut into small dice
1 onion, peeled and chopped
2 celery sticks, sliced
1 clove garlic, peeled and finely chopped
14 oz (400g) can flageolet beans
14 oz (400g) can chick peas, drained
14 oz (397g) can chopped tomatoes
Salt and pepper
1 teasp ground coriander
1 teasp ground cumin
1 teasp chilli powder
2 oz (50g) bulgar wheat

1. Put all the prepared vegetables, beans, plus liquor, drained chick peas, tomatoes, seasoning, spices and bulgar wheat in a saucepan.

2. Bring to the boil, stirring well, then simmer for about 20 minutes until the potato is tender.

7 FISH

For an island nation which invented the famous 'fish and chips', the British are notoriously squeamish when it comes to trying out new varieties of fish.

Be adventurous! Some of the more unusual fish now offered by fishmongers and the larger supermarkets are well worth trying, if only for convenience. Fish cooks quickly so is a boon to the after work cook.

Although dozens of interesting and exotic dishes can be made by combining fish with other ingredients, often the simplest is the nicest.

Try frying a slice of tuna, swordfish or shark in a little olive oil and a clove of finely chopped garlic. Serve sprinkled with lemon or lime juice, ground black pepper and a few chopped fresh herbs. A mixture of parsley and dill is particularly good, but fennel, chervil, lemon verbena or basil are all suitable.

Either accompany with a crisp green salad, or promote a Mediterranean flavour by frying a mixture of finely diced aubergine, green pepper and tomatoes alongside the fish.

MONKFISH KEBABS

The firm meaty texture of monkfish is not unlike lobster and is
excellent for kebabs. For economy, substitute halibut, or in-
tersperse the monkfish with chunks of vegetables. Allow about
1 lb (450g) of fish to serve four people. Cut the fish into bite-size
pieces, thread on skewers and grill for about 10 minutes, brushing
frequently with one of the following marinades.

SPICY MARINADE
2 tablsp cooking oil
Juice 1 lemon
Salt and pepper
2 teasp coriander seeds, crushed
1 teasp paprika
1 teasp Tabasco sauce

Combine all the ingredients.

GARLIC BUTTER
2 oz (50g) butter
1 clove garlic, peeled and finely chopped
Squeeze lemon juice
1 tablsp chopped parsley

Combine all the ingredients and spread on the kebabs. As the butter melts under the grill, brush the liquid frequently over the fish.

CANTONESE MARINADE
This gives a rather exotic flavour to fish.

4 tablsp cooking oil
3 tablsp white wine
2 teasp soy sauce
1 clove garlic, peeled and finely chopped
1 teasp dry ginger

Combine all the ingredients well.

FISH PROVENÇAL   *Serves 4*

A recipe with Greek origins. The lemon, garlic and tomatoes combine to make a tasty sauce in which the fish cooks.

Preparation time: 10 mins.   Cooking time: 25 mins.

1 onion, peeled and chopped
1 clove garlic, peeled and finely chopped
½ tablsp cooking oil
4 tomatoes, cut into pieces
Grated rind and juice of 1 lemon
Salt and pepper
1 lb (450g) white fish (cod, haddock, coley, etc.)

1.   Pre-heat oven to 190°C (375°F) or Gas No 5.

2.   Fry the onion and garlic in the oil until tender.

3.   Add the tomatoes, lemon rind and juice and seasoning.

4.   Wash and pat dry the fillets of fish and put them in a shallow ovenproof dish. Pour over the tomato mixture and bake in oven for about 15 minutes, depending on the thickness of the fish.

LIME AND CHILLI SOUSED
MACKEREL   *Serves 4*

The combination of tangy lime and hot chilli counteracts the richness of the mackerel well. The fish can be served hot, although personally I prefer it cold with salad and crusty bread and butter.

Preparation time: 8 mins.   Cooking time: 10 mins.
Marinading time: 30 mins. (if possible).

4 mackerel
Grated rind and juice of 1 lime
½ tablsp hot pepper OR chilli sauce

(continued overleaf)

(Lime and Chilli Soused Mackerel continued)

1 teasp soft brown sugar
Salt and pepper
2 tablsp chopped parsley for garnish (optional)

1. Although it is not difficult to bone mackerel, for quickness
    I usually ask my fishmonger to do the job. Using a sharp
    knife, score the mackerel at ½″ (1cm) intervals. Place the
    fish close together in a shallow dish.

2. Combine the grated rind and lime juice, pepper or chilli
    sauce, sugar and seasoning. Pour over the mackerel, brushing
    it well into the cuts. If possible leave to marinade for 30
    minutes.

3. Place the mackerel in a grill pan and grill under a medium
    heat for about 10 minutes. There is no need to turn the fish,
    but brush it frequently with the marinade.

4. If liked, the skin can be peeled off before serving. Garnish
    with chopped parsley.

NB Herrings could also be treated in this way.

MUSTARD AND YOGHURT-GLAZED
PLAICE   *Serves 4*

My husband, not the greatest of fish lovers, said how much he
enjoyed this recipe!

Preparation time: 4 mins.   Cooking time: 8 mins.

4 fillets plaice
Salt and pepper
Splash white wine OR milk
3 tablsp natural yoghurt
3 teasp French mustard
Grated Parmesan cheese

1. Pre-heat oven to 200°C (400°F) or Gas No 6.

2. Sprinkle the fillets with salt and pepper and place them in a shallow ovenproof dish. Pour in a splash of wine or milk just to cover the bottom of the dish.

3. Mix the yoghurt and mustard together and spread on the fish. Sprinkle with Parmesan cheese.

4. Bake in oven for about 8 minutes depending on thickness of the fish. Serve with sauté potatoes and green vegetables.

SOLE VERONIQUE   *Serves 4*

This is a classic dish traditionally made with, what is known in the trade as, allemande sauce. This is made with lemon juice, egg yolks, wine and cream. Here is my quick, and just as tasty, version using a packet sauce mix. For a special occasion you could add a few prawns with the grapes and serve in individual scallop shells as a starter.

Preparation time: 10 mins.   Cooking time: 20 mins.

4 fillets sole (plaice could be substituted)
4 oz (100g) white grapes
Salt and pepper
¼ pt (150ml) white wine
Packet (standard/25g size) Hollandaise sauce mix
   (makes ½ pint)
Milk

1. Pre-heat oven to 190°C (375°F) or Gas No 5.

2. Lay the fillets skin-side up on a board.

3. Halve the grapes and remove pips. (By rights the grapes should also be peeled but this is not essential.) Divide the grapes between the fillets and season well with salt and pepper.

4. Fold the fillets lengthwise into three and place them in a shallow ovenproof dish.

5. Pour on the wine, cover with foil and cook in oven for about 15 minutes, depending on thickness of the fish.

6. Drain the fish and keep warm. Make up the sauce mix according to manufacturer's instructions using the fish liquor, and milk if necessary to the required amount.

7. Pour the sauce over the fish and garnish with chopped parsley if liked.

PRAWN AND CASHEW STIR-FRY   *Serves 4*

This is a good recipe for making a few prawns go a long way. Serve with thin Chinese-style noodles.

Preparation time: 10 mins.   Cooking time: 15 mins.

1 onion, peeled and chopped
4 courgettes, sliced
4 oz (100g) mushrooms, sliced
2 tablsp cooking oil
8 oz (225g) beansprouts
Juice 1 lemon
1 tablsp soy sauce
3 oz (75g) cashew nuts
8 oz (225g) peeled prawns

1. Fry the onion, courgettes and mushrooms in the oil for about 10 minutes.

2. Stir in the beansprouts, lemon juice, soy sauce, cashew nuts and prawns and cook for a further 5 minutes.

PRAWN CREOLE   *Serves 3-4*

Be warned — this is a real hot one! It's a throw-it-all-in-a-saucepan recipe and excellent served with garlic bread and green salad.

Preparation time: 10 mins.   Cooking time: 20 mins.

Packet (5 oz/120g size) curry-flavoured rice
4 fresh chillies, chopped
8 oz (225g) broccoli, cut into small florets
14 oz (397g) can chopped tomatoes
Juice 1 lemon
8 oz (225g) peeled prawns
5 fl oz (150ml) carton soured cream (optional)

1. Put the rice in a saucepan with water according to manufacturer's instructions. (Follow exactly so there will be little or no liquid at the end.)

2. Simmer gently for 10 minutes then add the chillies and broccoli and complete the cooking time.

3. Stir in the tomatoes, lemon juice, prawns and soured cream, if using. Heat for a further couple of minutes.

COQUILLES ST JACQUES

Serves 4 as a starter or 2 as a main course

Delicately flavoured and firm-textured scallops are unfortunately expensive. Although in season from October to March they are now widely available frozen. This recipe is perhaps too costly for family meals, but if you are entertaining, scallops make a delicious main course or starter. To make the scallops go further, combine with other firm fleshed white fish and a few prawns to make a wonderful seafood medley.

Preparation time: 5 mins.   Cooking time: 10 mins.

Handful dried sliced mushrooms
8 scallops
¼ pt (150ml) white wine
Shake salt
Freshly ground black pepper

(continued overleaf)

(Coquilles St Jacques continued)

Piece raw onion, peeled
1 tablsp flour
1 tablsp butter or margarine
2-3 tablsp single cream
Grated Parmesan cheese

1. Put the dried mushrooms in a cup and pour on boiling water.

2. Put the scallops, wine, salt, pepper and onion in a small pan.
    Bring to the boil and simmer for about 5 minutes until the
    scallops are tender.

3. Meanwhile blend the flour and butter or margarine in a small
    bowl.

4. Lift out the scallops with a slotted spoon and place them in
    a warm serving dish or individual scallop shells. Drain the
    mushrooms and scatter over.

5. Add the blended flour and butter to the scallop liquor and stir
    over a medium heat until thickened. Stir in the cream and
    adjust seasoning.

6. Pour the sauce over the scallops, sprinkle liberally with grated
    Parmesan cheese and brown under a hot grill for a couple of
    minutes.

POACHED FRESH SALMON

Largely due to fish farming, salmon is one of the few foods which
has dropped in price in recent years. It is now almost half the cost
of fillet steak and, according to the experts, is infinitely healthier.
Research shows that the fatty acids, known as omega 3s, which
are concentrated in cold water fish, help protect against a long
string of diseases including blood clotting and strokes.

Salmon is usually sold in middle steaks or cutlets, or tail end
fillets. Allow about 4 oz (100g) per person.

Preparation time: 5 mins.   Cooking time: 10 mins.

Water
Piece raw peeled onion
6 peppercorns
Bay leaf
1 teasp salt
Juice 1 lemon

1. Place the salmon in a saucepan with enough water to barely cover it. (A mixture of water and white wine can be used if preferred.)

2. Add the remainder of the ingredients, bring to the boil then simmer gently for about 10 minutes. Unless serving hot, allow the salmon to cool in the liquor. Peel off the skin and discard.

The delicate flavour of this unique fish needs little or no embellishment making it an ideal choice for the after work cook. The exception perhaps is French mayonnaise or an alternative good quality side-of-plate dressing. Here are two of my favourites.

WATERCRESS MOUSSELINE   *Serves 4*

Preparation time: 5 mins.

1 bunch watercress
3 tablsp double cream
3 tablsp French-style mayonnaise
Salt and black pepper
Juice ½ lemon

1. Cut the stalks off the watercress and chop the leaves.

2. Mix the leaves, cream, mayonnaise, seasoning and lemon juice well together.

RASPBERRY AND CRANBERRY SAUCE *Serves 4*

Preparation time: 2 mins.   Cooking time: 5 mins.

4 oz (100g) raspberries
2 tablsp cranberry jelly
Juice ½ lemon

Put the three ingredients into a small pan and heat gently until
the cranberry jelly melts. Boil for about 5 minutes until the
liquid has reduced and thickened. Mash the raspberries lightly
and leave in the fridge until cold.

SALMON KEDGEREE   *Serves 3-4*

This delicately flavoured and delicious kedgeree is ideal for a light
supper. Its economical use of salmon makes it light on the pocket
too. For quickness you can use canned salmon but surprisingly
there is little difference in cost. Fresh dill is by far superior to dried
in this recipe but if you can't get it, use a bunch of chopped
watercress leaves instead. Serve with crusty bread and a tomato
salad.

Preparation time: 8 mins.   Cooking time: 35 mins.

8 oz (225g) wild rice (see page 53)
½ teasp salt
½ cucumber, peeled and diced
Juice 1 lemon
1 tablsp chopped fresh dill
Freshly ground black pepper
8 oz (225g) cold cooked salmon OR 1 (7½ oz/213g) can,
    drained and flaked
Wafer thin slices onion for garnish (optional)

1. Cook the rice according to the manufacturer's instructions,
    using the stated amount of water.

2. Add salt, cucumber, lemon juice, dill, pepper and salmon.
    Serve warm or cold and garnish with onion if liked.

TUNA AND BROCCOLI MORNAY   *Serves 3-4*

This tasty dish could be made with salmon but tuna is cheaper.
Serve with savoury rice.

Preparation time: 10 mins.   Cooking time: 30 mins.

1 lb (450g) broccoli, fresh or frozen
Packet Hollandaise sauce mix
½ pt (300ml) milk
Large (14 oz/397g) can tuna fish OR 15½ oz (440g) salmon,
  drained and flaked
2 oz (50g) mature Cheddar cheese, grated

1. Pre-heat oven to 190°C (375°F) or Gas No 5.

2. Break the broccoli into florets and cook in boiling salted water
    for 8-10 minutes until just tender. Drain.

3. Meanwhile make up the Hollandaise sauce with the milk
    according to manufacturer's instructions.

4. Put the drained broccoli and the flaked tuna or salmon into
    a shallow ovenproof dish and pour over the sauce.

5. Top with grated cheese and bake in oven for about 20 minutes
    until brown and bubbly.

SMOKED HADDOCK FRICASSEE   *Serves 4*

The combination of orange and Worcestershire sauce creates a nice
flavour which tempts children if they're not too keen on fish.

Preparation time: 8 mins.   Cooking time: 10 mins.

12 oz (350g) smoked haddock
¼ pt (150ml) milk
Salt and pepper
Handful frozen peas

(continued overleaf)

(Smoked Haddock Fricassee continued)

Small (11 oz/312g) can mandarin oranges
1 tablsp Worcestershire sauce
Packet (standard/17g size) white sauce mix (makes ½ pint)
7 oz (200g) can sweetcorn, drained

1. Poach the haddock in the milk and seasoning for about 6 minutes until the fish flakes easily.

2. Put the peas in a cup and pour on boiling water.

3. Blend 3 tablespoons of mandarin juice and the Worcestershire sauce with the sauce mix in a small pan.

4. Drain the fish, reserving the liquor. Remove skin and any bones and flake the flesh into a bowl.

5. Add the fish liquor to the sauce mix, bring to the boil and stir until thickened.

6. Mix the fish, sauce, drained peas, oranges and sweetcorn together and sprinkle with chopped parsley if liked. Serve with savoury rice.

SARDINES EN PAPILOTTE   *Serves 4*

Sardines and trout are particularly good cooked in the French way, which literally means fish cooked in paper. Use greaseproof or foil and there isn't even any washing up! Supermarket fish departments or fishmongers will prepare the fish for you. Personal preference will dictate whether or not you leave on the heads.

Preparation time: 5 mins.   Cooking time: 20 mins.

8-12 fresh sardines
Salt and pepper
Juice 1 lemon
Roughly chopped herbs — parsley, dill, fennel or chives
1 courgette, sliced OR thick slices cucumber
2 tomatoes, sliced

1. Pre-heat oven to 190°C (375°F) or Gas No 5.

2. Brush four squares of greaseproof or foil with oil and put 2-3 washed sardines on each.

3. Sprinkle with salt and pepper, lemon juice and chopped herbs. Lay the slices of courgette, or cucumber, and tomato on top and season again.

4. Fold the paper around the sardines into individual parcels and bake in the oven for about 20 minutes until the sardines and vegetables are tender. Serve with salad and savoury rice.

HADDOCK IN MUSHROOM SAUCE   *Serves 4*

Nothing could be quicker or easier to prepare. The mushroom soup forms a tasty coating-sauce and most varieties of white fish are suitable. For an even quicker version, omit the onion and heat a can of flaked tuna fish in the soup. Serve with savoury rice or matchstick fried potatoes and peas or tomatoes.

Preparation time: 5 mins.   Cooking time: 25 mins.

1 onion, peeled and chopped
6 oz (175g) mushrooms, sliced
4 fillets haddock
10.4 oz (295g) can condensed mushroom soup
3 tablsp milk
Chopped parsley for garnish (optional)

1. Pre-heat oven to 190°C (375°F) or Gas No 5.

2. Put the onion and mushrooms in a shallow ovenproof dish and lay the fish on top.

3. Pour on the soup and milk and give the dish a good shake to mix the liquids.

4. Cover with foil and cook for about 25 minutes until the fish and vegetables are tender. (Halfway through cooking, give

the dish another shake and remove the foil for the last 5 minutes.)

5.   If liked, garnish with chopped parsley.

HADDOCK AND PRAWN CROISSANTS   *Serves 4*

Prawns add a touch of luxury to this recipe but make a more economical version by substituting a few cooked peas and/or some drained sweetcorn.

Preparation time: 5 mins.   Cooking time: 15 mins.

12 oz (350g) haddock fillets
½ pt (300ml) milk
Salt and pepper
4 croissants
Packet Hollandaise sauce mix
4 oz (100g) peeled prawns

1.   Put the fish, milk and seasoning in a saucepan, bring to the boil and simmer gently for about 10 minutes until the fish is tender.

2.   Slice the croissants in two horizontally but do not separate. Place on a baking tray and heat in a warm oven for 5 minutes.

3.   Drain the fish, reserving the liquor. Remove skin if liked and roughly flake the flesh.

4.   Make up the sauce mix, according to manufacturer's instructions, using the fish liquor.

5.   Stir in fish and prawns.

6.   Place each bottom half croissant on a plate, spoon on some fish mixture and top with the other half croissant.

Serve with a selection of vegetables cooked until just tender. Green beans, carrots and leeks are a good choice.

SEAFOOD VOL-AU-VENTS
Serves 4

The preparation for this dish can be done while the vol-au-vents
are cooking, thus saving further time. If possible, use cooked fresh
mussels which are usually available from fish departments of large
supermarkets. If not, buy the mussels bottled in brine.

Preparation time: 10 mins.   Cooking time: 12 mins.

4 king-size frozen vol-au-vents
Packet (standard/17g size) white sauce mix (makes ½ pint)
½ pt (300ml) milk
2 oz (50g) peeled prawns
2 oz (50g) cooked fresh mussels
7 oz (200g) can tuna fish, drained and flaked
7 oz (200g) can sweetcorn, drained
Swig sherry
Ground black pepper

1. Pre-heat oven to 220°C (425°F) or Gas No 7. Cook the vol-
    au-vents in the oven for about 12 minutes until well risen and
    lightly brown.

2. Meanwhile make up the sauce with the milk according to
    manufacturer's instructions.

3. Stir in the prawns, mussels, tuna fish, corn, sherry and
    pepper. Mix well.

4. Remove the lids from the vol-au-vents and pull out and discard
    uncooked pastry.

5. Fill the vol-au-vents with the fish mixture, pop on the lids and
    heat in the oven for 3 minutes.

    Serve with salad and some sliced chicory tossed in vinaigrette
    dressing.

SQUID STIR-FRY

Serves 4

A friend's husband kindly donated this recipe. (She said it was the only meal he ever cooked!) Squid is usually cut into rings but this method is more attractive and nicer to eat. The fish combines well with lightly cooked vegetables into a meal which is full of texture and flavour.

Preparation time: 15 mins.   Cooking time: 10 mins.

1½ lb (700g) small squid
2 tablsp cooking oil
2 tablsp soy sauce
2 cloves garlic, peeled and crushed
½ teasp chilli powder
8 oz (225g) broccoli, cut into small florets
4 oz (100g) mushrooms, sliced
1 carrot, grated

1. Cut off the tentacles below the ink sac. Split the squid down the side and flatten out. Scrape out innards, ink sac and skin. You should be left with flat fillets.

2. With a sharp knife lightly score the fillets diagonally in both directions. Cut each squid into about four pieces. Wash and dry thoroughly.

3. Heat the oil, soy sauce, garlic and chilli powder in a wok or large frying pan.

4. Add the squid and the tentacles to the hot liquid and stir over a fairly high heat for 5 minutes.

5. Stir in the broccoli, mushrooms and carrot and continue stir frying for a further 5 minutes.

    Serve with rice.

8 MEAT

KEBABS

Kebabs make a quick meal and are especially delicious when marinaded in a tasty or spicy mixture before cooking. If you can spare 10 minutes the previous evening to prepare the marinade, all you have to do the following night is thread the meat on the skewers and throw them under the grill!

If energy and time are short, just rub the kebabs with a cut clove of garlic, trickle with lemon juice and season. Choose a selection of meat from the following:

Leg or fillet of lamb
Pork tenderloin
Rump or fillet steak
Boneless and skinless chicken portions
King prawns
Pieces of good butcher's sausage or Cumberland sausage
Liver, kidneys, bacon rolls

Allow about 4-6 oz (100-175g) meat per person and cut it into bite-size pieces before marinading. Good, and therefore expensive, cuts of meat must be used for grilling but it can be 'stretched' with the addition of certain vegetables:

Chunks of red, green and yellow peppers
Pieces of marrow
Quarters of par-boiled onion
Chunks of aubergine
Courgettes, cut into three or four pieces
Small whole tomatoes
Button mushrooms

Use long metal or wooden skewers and cook under a medium grill, turning occasionally and brushing frequently with the marinade, or a little oil.

Kebabs are especially good served with wild rice and a salad tossed in a vinaigrette dressing.

MEDITERRANEAN MARINADE
(good with pork and lamb)

4 tablsp cooking oil
4 tablsp sherry
1 clove garlic, peeled and chopped
2 tablsp chopped fresh parsley
1 tablsp chopped fresh oregano or 1 teasp dried
Salt and pepper

Combine all the ingredients and marinade the meat overnight if possible.

LAMB OR CHICKEN TIKKA   *Serves 4*

This marinade has a thick consistency so doesn't really need to be left overnight.

Preparation time: 10 mins.   Cooking time: 15 mins.

1 lb (450g) leg or fillet of lamb
1 small onion, peeled and finely chopped
1 clove garlic, peeled and finely chopped
Juice 1 lemon
1 tablsp cooking oil
2 tablsp tomato purée
2 teasp ground coriander
1 teasp turmeric
1 teasp chilli powder
½ tablsp hot pepper or chilli sauce (optional)

1. Cut the lamb into bite-size pieces. (Chicken can be used if preferred.)

2. Mix the remaining ingredients together and stir in the meat.

3. Thread the meat on skewers, spoon over remaining marinade and cook under a medium grill for about 15 minutes, turning occasionally.

SATAY KEBABS
(good with any of the meat listed on page 81)

Juice 1 lemon
1 clove garlic, peeled and chopped
1 tablsp chopped fresh mixed herbs OR 1 teasp dried
3 tablsp crunchy peanut butter
½ stock cube made with ¼ pt (150ml) water
1 onion, peeled and finely chopped

1. Marinade the meat in the lemon juice, garlic and mixed herbs and leave overnight.

2. The next evening blend the peanut butter with the stock, onion and a little of the lemon marinade to give a coating consistency.

3. Thread the meat on skewers and spoon over the peanut mixture.

4. Cook under a gentle grill, turning occasionally and spooning on more of the peanut mixture.

CHINESE MARINADE
(good with all the meat listed on page 81)

2 tablsp soy sauce
1 tablsp cooking oil
Juice ½ lemon
1 teasp soft brown sugar
1 clove garlic, peeled and chopped
Knob fresh ginger, peeled and grated OR ½ teasp
**   ground ginger**

Combine all the ingredients well and marinade meat for several hours if possible.

MARYLAND KEBABS   *Serves 4*

Preparation time: 15 mins.   Cooking time: 20 mins.

6-8 boneless and skinless chicken thighs
1 tablsp soft brown sugar
1 tablsp Worcestershire sauce
Juice 1 lemon
4 rashers smoked streaky bacon
2 bananas

1. Cut each chicken thigh into four pieces.

2. Blend the sugar, Worcestershire sauce and lemon juice in a small bowl and stir in the chicken. Leave to marinade overnight.

3. The next evening cut the bacon rashers in two and the bananas into four pieces.

4. Wrap a piece of bacon around each piece of banana.

5. Thread the chicken and the bacon-wrapped bananas on skewers, brush well with the marinade and grill gently for about 10 minutes on each side.

SHEEK KEBABS   *Serves 4*

Preparation time: 15 mins.   Cooking time: 15 mins.

1 lb (450g) best minced beef
3 cloves garlic, peeled and finely chopped
Knob fresh ginger, peeled and grated
2 fresh chillies, finely chopped, OR 1 teasp dried crushed
    chillies
2 teasp ground coriander
1 tablsp curry paste or powder
1 egg, beaten

1. Mix all the ingredients together, using your hand if necessary
    to bind well.

2. With floured hands form the mixture into sausage shapes
    about 3″ (7½cm) long and thread two or three on each
    skewer.

3. Brush with oil and grill gently for about 15 minutes, turning
    occasionally. Serve hot or cold with Mustard Sauce (page
    86).

SAUSAGE HERB AND GARLIC KEBABS *Serves 4*

This mixture can either be made into kebabs and served as a main
course, or formed into balls (makes 40) and fried. They can be
speared on cocktail sticks and handed round as 'nibbles' for bon-
fire night celebrations, Christmas and New Year get-togethers,
or indeed any party occasion.

Preparation time: 15 mins.   Cooking time: 15 mins.

1 lb (450g) pork sausagemeat
4 oz (100g) packet herb and garlic stuffing mix
1 egg, beaten

1. Mix all the ingredients well together, using your hand if
    necessary.

2.   Flour your hands and, if making kebabs, form the mixture
     into sausage shapes. If making party 'nibbles' roll the mixture
     into small balls.

3.   Thread the kebabs on metal or wooden skewers and grill for
     about 15 minutes turning frequently. Fry the balls in hot oil
     for about 10 minutes and drain on kitchen paper. Serve
     with .....

MUSTARD SAUCE

Preparation time: 8 mins.

6 tablsp mayonnaise
2 teasp English mustard
1 teasp lemon juice
1 teasp tomato ketchup
2 teasp Worcestershire sauce

   Combine all the ingredients into a smooth cream.

PORK KEBABS WITH APRICOTS AND PINEAPPLE   *Serves 4*

Fruit goes particularly well with pork because it counteracts the
rich meat.

Preparation time: 10 mins.   Cooking time: 20-25 mins.

1 lb (450g) pork tenderloin
8 dried apricots
8 oz (225g) can pineapple chunks
1 tablsp cooking oil
1 tablsp soy sauce
Knob fresh ginger, peeled and grated

1.   Cut pork into bite-size pieces.

2.   Put pork, apricots, pineapple and juice, oil, soy sauce and

ginger into a bowl. Stir well and leave to marinade overnight.

3. Thread meat and fruit alternately on skewers, brush with marinade and cook under a medium grill, turning occasionally, for 20-25 minutes.

CHICKEN LIME KEBABS
Serves 4

A delicious sweet and sour marinade.

Preparation time: 6 mins.   Cooking time: 15 mins.

8 boneless and skinless chicken thighs
1 tablsp tomato purée
Juice 1 lime
1 tablsp cooking oil
½ tablsp Worcestershire sauce
2 tablsp lime marmalade
1 clove garlic, peeled and chopped

1. Cut each chicken thigh into four.

2. Blend the remaining ingredients well together and marinade the chicken overnight.

3. Thread the chicken on skewers, brush with the marinade and grill for about 15 minutes, turning occasionally.

LIVER AND BACON KEBABS
Serves 4

The combination of liver and bacon is a traditional favourite. Try this tasty way of cooking for a change.

Preparation time: 8 mins.   Cooking time: 10 mins.

1 lb (450g) lamb's liver
6 oz (175g) smoked streaky bacon
4 oz (100g) button mushrooms

(continued overleaf)

(Liver and Bacon Kebabs continued)

Juice 1 lemon
Salt and ground black pepper
Cooking oil

1.   Cut the liver into ½" (1cm) pieces.

2.   Cut the rashers of bacon into two and roll up each piece.

3.   Thread the liver, bacon rolls and mushrooms alternately on
     skewers and sprinkle with lemon juice, salt and pepper.

4.   Brush with oil and cook under a medium grill for about 10
     minutes, turning once.

     Serve with savoury rice and salad.

DEVILLED KIDNEY KEBABS   *Serves 4*

Kidneys are tender if cooked quickly which makes them ideal for
the after work cook. This spicy way of serving should appeal to
those members of the family who perhaps are not usually keen on
kidneys.

Preparation time: 8 mins.   Cooking time: 10 mins.

10-12 lamb's kidneys
1 teasp salt
½ teasp cayenne pepper
2 teasp mustard powder
2 teasp curry powder

1.   Split the kidneys without actually dividing them. Using
     scissors, remove the white core and as many tubes as possible.

2.   Make several slashes in the kidneys with a sharp knife.

3.   Mix the salt, cayenne, mustard and curry powder together and
     rub into the kidneys.

4. Thread on skewers, brush with oil and cook under medium
    grill for about 5 minutes each side.

    Serve with croûtons of fried bread and a tomato and chicory
    salad trickled with vinaigrette dressing.

STIR-FRIES

Stir-fry dishes offer unlimited scope for quick and tasty meals.
They are made, as the name implies, by stirring and frying and
are great for using up bits and pieces. That chunk of green pepper,
for example, which has been lying in the fridge for days, the odd
banana which no-one is willing to eat, or the half used can of
pineapple.

Pre-packaged and frozen stir-fry vegetables are now available
from most supermarkets. They usually contain a combination of
beansprouts, courgettes, onion, peppers, sweetcorn, mushrooms
and water chestnuts. For quickness these are well worth using, but
by preparing your own vegetables you can choose particular family
favourites. Of the recipes listed here, one includes a pre-packaged
mixture and five give ideas for home prepared veg.

Apart from the varieties already mentioned, most vegetables
are suitable, including aubergine, cabbage, carrots, marrow, leeks,
tomatoes, broccoli and sliced green beans.

By increasing or decreasing the meat content, stir-fry meals can
be as expensive or as economical as you wish to make them. Meat
quantities in the following recipes are given only as a suggestion.

Allow 1 lb-1¼ lb (450g-575g) of mixed vegetables if the dish
contains meat, but about 2 lb (900g) if using vegetables only. (See
also chapters on Fish and Vegetables.) Soya products like tofu can
be stir-fried and substituted for meat or fish if liked.

Stir-fry meals are traditionally cooked in a Chinese wok, but
a large frying pan will do. If possible, use sesame seed oil as it
imparts an authentic seasoning and flavour.

CARIBBEAN STIR-FRY   *Serves 4*

The addition of mango and banana conveys an exotic flavour to
this quickly made chicken dish.

Preparation time: 10 mins.   Cooking time: 15 mins.

10-12 oz (275g-350g) boneless and skinless chicken
Salt and pepper
2 tablsp sesame seed oil
1 onion, peeled and chopped
1 red pepper, de-seeded and sliced
2 courgettes, sliced
2 tablsp soy sauce
1 mango, peeled and sliced
1 banana, peeled and sliced
10 oz (275g) carton beansprouts
1 tablsp flaked almonds (optional)

1. Thinly slice the chicken and season with salt and pepper.

2. Fry quickly in the hot oil until sealed on both sides.

3. Add the onion, pepper, courgettes and soy sauce and stir-fry
    for about 10 minutes.

4. Add the mango, banana and beansprouts and fry for a further
    5 minutes.

5. Serve sprinkled with flaked almonds if liked.

INDIAN STIR-FRY   *Serves 4*

Use boneless and skinless chicken or pork tenderloin in this subtly
spiced recipe. Add a little chilli powder if you prefer a distinct
'kick'. Serve with rice.

Preparation time: 10 mins.   Cooking time: 15 mins.

10-12 oz (275g-350g) chicken or pork
3 tablsp sesame seed oil
1 tablsp curry paste
4 oz (100g) mushrooms, sliced

1 aubergine, diced
1 onion, peeled and chopped
4 tomatoes, cut into pieces
2 tablsp sultanas
Desiccated coconut for garnish (optional)

1. Slice the chicken or pork.

2. Heat the oil and curry paste and fry the meat quickly until
    sealed.

3. Add the vegetables and sultanas and stir-fry for about 15
    minutes. (Aubergines absorb lots of oil so add a little more
    if the mixture looks too dry.) Serve sprinkled with coconut
    if liked.

CHINESE STIR-FRY   *Serves 4*

This recipe uses ready-prepared stir-fry vegetables which cuts
down preparation time.

Preparation time: 5 mins.   Cooking time: 15 mins.

10-12 oz (275g-350g) chicken or pork
Salt and pepper
2 tablsp sesame seed oil
1 onion, peeled and chopped
1 tablsp soy sauce
8 oz (225g) can pineapple pieces
1 lb (450g) pack stir-fry vegetables

1. Slice the chicken or pork and season.

2. Fry the meat quickly in the hot oil until sealed on both sides.

3. Add the onion and soy sauce and stir-fry for about 10 minutes,
    until the meat is tender.

5. Add the pineapple pieces with a couple of tablespoons of juice,
    and the vegetables. Stir-fry for a further 5 minutes.

JAPANESE BEEF
Serves 4

Remember the better quality of steak used, the better the finished result will be!

Preparation time: 10 mins.   Cooking time: 15 mins.

10-12 oz (275-350g) frying steak, rump or fillet
Salt and pepper
2 tablsp sesame seed oil
Knob fresh ginger, peeled and grated
2 tablsp soy sauce
1 tablsp clear honey
2 tablsp sherry
1 onion, peeled and chopped
8 oz (225g) fresh or frozen green beans
8 oz (225g) leeks, sliced thinly
10 oz (275g) carton beansprouts

1. Cut the meat into strips and season with salt and pepper.

2. Fry the meat quickly in the hot oil until sealed on both sides.

3. Stir in the ginger, soy sauce, honey, sherry and the vegetables.

S. Stir-fry for about 10 minutes, depending on how rare or well done you like your steak.

   Serve with savoury rice.

COLIN'S CHICKEN STIR-FRY
Serves 4

This recipe uses half a head of Chinese leaves. Use the remainder in a salad or cook for a few minutes in boiling salted water, drain and top with a cheese sauce. Serve another night as an accompaniment to cold meat.

Preparation time: 8 mins.   Cooking time: 10 mins.

1 tablsp sesame seed oil
1 tablsp soy sauce
½ teasp chilli powder
1 clove garlic, peeled and crushed
12 oz (350g) boneless and skinless chicken breast or thighs,
    cut into bite-size pieces
8 oz (225g) broccoli, cut into small florets
4 oz (100g) mushrooms, sliced
½ head Chinese leaves, sliced
1 green pepper, de-seeded and chopped
Salt and pepper

1. Heat the oil, soy sauce and chilli powder in a wok or large
    frying pan.

2. Add the garlic and chicken and stir-fry for 5 minutes.

3. Add all the vegetables, season and stir-fry for a further 5
    minutes. The vegetables should be crunchy to eat.

    Serve with savoury rice.

LAMB WITH GARLIC   *Serves 4*

Succulent pieces of lamb are cooked in their own juices with garlic,
soy sauce, sherry and tooth-tender celery and courgettes. Serve
with rice.

Preparation time: 10 mins.   Cooking time: 20 mins.

1 tablsp sesame seed oil
3 cloves garlic, peeled and finely chopped
1 onion, peeled and chopped
1 lb (450g) lean lamb (leg or fillet), cut into pieces
¼ teasp chilli powder
Salt and pepper
1 tablsp soy sauce
1 tablsp sherry
2 sticks celery, sliced
2 medium courgettes, cut into strips

1. Heat the oil in a wok or large frying pan, add the garlic, onion, lamb, chilli powder and seasoning and stir-fry until the meat has browned, about 5 minutes.

2. Stir in the soy sauce, sherry, celery and courgettes and cook for about 15 minutes, stirring frequently, until the meat is tender.

GAMMON

Gammon makes a change and is quick and easy to cook too. Big supermarkets sell smoked tendersweet bacon chops and loin roasts, which although not cheap, are lean, full of flavour and there is no waste. The following recipes can be made using either bacon chops, loin roast (allow about 2 slices per person) or the more usual gammon steak.

BACON CHOPS WITH CREAMY MUSHROOMS
Serves 4

My son said that this was the nicest recipe in the book. A back-handed compliment perhaps seeing his favourite foods are beefburgers and pizza! (See page 23 for serving one or two.)

Preparation time: 10 mins.   Cooking time: 20 mins.

4 bacon chops
1 onion, peeled and chopped
4 oz (100g) mushrooms, sliced
1 tablsp tomato purée
7 fl oz (200ml) white wine
¼ pt (150ml) double cream
Grated Parmesan cheese (optional)

1. Grill the bacon chops for about 10 minutes on each side. Transfer to a shallow ovenproof dish.

2. Meanwhile put the onion, mushrooms, tomato purée and wine in a small saucepan. Simmer until tender, about 10 minutes.

3. Boil rapidly for a further five minutes until the liquid has reduced.

4. Stir in the cream and pour the sauce over the chops.

5. If liked sprinkle with Parmesan cheese and brown under a hot grill.

DEVILLED GAMMON
Serves 4

A variation on the perennial favourite — gammon with pineapple. Brown sugar and mustard make the dish a little more interesting.

Preparation time: 5 mins.   Cooking time: 20-30 mins.

4 gammon steaks
4 teasp mustard
4 teasp soft brown sugar
8 oz (225g) can pineapple rings

1. Place the gammon on a sheet of foil in the grill pan.

2. Mix the mustard, brown sugar and a couple of tablespoons of pineapple juice together. Pour half the mixture on the gammon and grill for 10-15 minutes.

3. Turn the gammon over, pour on the remaining mixture and repeat the cooking time.

4. Top each gammon steak with a pineapple ring and and trickle over the rest of the pineapple juice. Grill for a couple of minutes to heat through.

CHEESE-TOPPED GAMMON
Serves 4

Gruyère cheese imparts a more interesting flavour, but children may prefer processed cheese slices.

Preparation time: 2 mins.   Cooking time: 30 mins.

4 gammon steaks
8 oz (225g) can pineapple rings
Slices Gruyère or processed cheese

1. Grill the gammon for about 10-15 minutes on each side.

2. Top with a pineapple ring and cover with slices of cheese. Grill until golden and bubbly.

GAMMON INDIENNE   *Serves 4*

Sweet and sour with a sting!

Preparation time: 4 mins.   Cooking time: 30 mins.

4 gammon steaks
2 tablsp clear honey
2 tablsp orange marmalade
1 tablsp Tabasco sauce

1. Pre-heat oven to 190°C (375°F) or Gas No 5.

2. Place the gammon on foil in a shallow ovenproof dish and cook for 10 minutes.

3. Mix the honey, marmalade and Tabasco together and spoon over the gammon. Cook for a further 20 minutes.

SWEET AND SOUR BACON CHOPS   *Serves 4*

Baked tomatoes and buttered new potatoes make good accompaniments.

Preparation time: 4 mins.   Cooking time: 30 mins.

4 bacon chops or slices tendersweet loin roast
2 tablsp clear honey

1 teasp mustard
2 teasp soy sauce

1. Place the chops or loin roast on a sheet of foil in a shallow ovenproof dish.

2. Mix the honey, mustard and soy sauce together and brush half of it over the meat. Grill for 15 minutes.

3. Turn and brush on the remaining honey mixture and grill for a further 15 minutes.

GAMMON MARSALA *Serves 4*

The rather sweet sherry-like liquid imparts a lovely flavour to this cream sauce. (See page 23, for serving one or two.)

Preparation time: 10 mins.   Cooking time: 20-30 mins.

4 gammon steaks
1 onion, peeled and chopped
1 clove garlic, peeled and finely chopped
4 oz (100g) mushrooms, sliced
1 tablsp cooking oil
¼ pt (150ml) Marsala
¼ pt (150ml) double cream
Salt and pepper
Chopped fresh parsley for garnish (optional)

1. Grill the gammon for about 15 minutes on each side.

2. Meanwhile, fry the onion, garlic and mushrooms in the oil until tender.

3. Add the Marsala and boil for about 5 minutes until reduced slightly. Stir in the cream and season to taste.

4. Pour the sauce over the gammon and sprinkle with chopped parsley if liked.

GAMMON WITH PLUM RELISH   *Serves 4*

A no-hassle tangy and fruity relish is just the thing with gammon.
(See page 23, for serving one or two.)

Preparation time: 5 mins.   Cooking time: 20 mins.

1 onion, peeled and chopped
3 plums, halved, de-stoned and sliced
½ tablsp cooking oil
2 tablsp sultanas
2 tablsp demerara sugar
Salt and pepper
4 fl oz (100ml) red wine vinegar
4 fl oz (100ml) water
4 gammon steaks

1. Fry the onion and sliced plums gently in the oil for 5 minutes.

2. Add the sultanas, sugar, seasoning, vinegar and water.

3. Boil for about 20 minutes until the relish is thick and syrupy.

4. Meanwhile, cook the gammon steaks under a medium grill
    for about 8 minutes on each side.

    Spoon over the relish and serve with new potatoes, peas and
    carrots.

HAM AND ASPARAGUS AU GRATIN   *Serves 4*

Packet mixes are useful for making sauces quickly. I don't find the
cheese variety very nice so I generally use the white sauce and add
freshly grated cheese. For economy, canned celery can be
substituted for asparagus.

Preparation time: 15 mins.   Cooking time: 20 mins.

**12 oz (340g) can asparagus spears or 1 lb 12 oz (794g) can
celery hearts**
6-8 slices cooked ham
Packet (standard/17g size) white sauce mix (makes ½ pint)
¼ pt (150ml) asparagus or celery juice
¼ pt (150ml) milk
4 oz (100g) mature Cheddar cheese, grated
Salt and pepper

1. Pre-heat oven to 180°C (350°F) or Gas No 4.

2. Drain the asparagus or celery, reserving the juice.

3. Divide the vegetables equally between each slice of ham and
    roll up. Place in a shallow ovenproof dish.

4. Make up the sauce mix according to manufacturer's
    instructions, using the vegetable juice and milk.

5. Add three quarters of the grated cheese and stir over a low
    heat until melted. Season to taste with salt and pepper.

6. Pour the sauce over the ham, sprinkle with the remaining
    cheese and bake for 20 minutes until nicely browned.

PORK, LAMB AND BEEF

PORK ROYALE *Serves 4-6*

Everyone has their 'pet' recipe and this is mine! The dish is ideal
for a dinner party if you haven't much time. The impressive result
belies the time it takes to prepare and cook. The sauce can be made
the night before and the cream added at the last minute. (See page
23, for serving one or two.)

Preparation time: 10 mins.   Cooking time: 30 mins.

1 lb-1½lb (450g-700g) pork tenderloin
Knob butter or margarine
1 onion, peeled and chopped

(continued overleaf)

(Pork Royale continued)

6 oz (175g) mushrooms, sliced
1 tablsp cooking oil
14 oz (397g) can tomatoes, drained
2 tablsp red wine (optional)
2 beef stock cubes
¼ pt (150ml) double cream
Freshly chopped parsley for garnish (optional)

1. Pre-heat oven to 180°C (350°F) or Gas No 4.

2. Cut pork into medallions, place on a sheet of foil and dot with butter. Make a parcel with the foil and roast in oven for about 30 minutes, opening the foil for the last 5 minutes.

3. Meanwhile, fry the onion and mushrooms in the oil until tender. Drain off excess juices.

4. Add drained tomatoes, chopping them a bit in the pan, the wine (if using) and crumble in the stock cubes. Stir over a low heat until dissolved and well mixed.

5. Pour in the cream and gently shake the pan to blend with the other ingredients. Do not boil.

6. Place the pork in a shallow serving dish and pour over the sauce. Garnish with chopped parsley if liked. Serve with savoury rice or scrubbed new potatoes in their jackets, and a green vegetable.

PORK WITH CIDER SAUCE   *Serves 4*

For recipes of this type which are being served with a tasty sauce, you can get away with the cheaper, thinner chops. These are ideal for the after work cook because they cook more quickly.

Preparation time: 3 mins.   Cooking time: 30 mins.

4 thin boneless pork chops
Salt and freshly ground black pepper
1 tablsp English mustard
1-2 tablsp oil
½ pt (300ml) medium sweet cider
Chopped fresh sage for garnish (optional)

1.   Season the chops and spread a little mustard on each.

2.   Fry the chops gently in the oil for about 10-15 minutes on each
     side. Remove to a warm serving dish.

3.   Pour the cider into the pan juices and boil until reduced and
     thickened. Pour over the chops and garnish with chopped sage
     if liked.

PORK CHOPS WITH MUSTARD CREAM SAUCE
Serves 4

Chops are usually expensive so the next time you shop look for
the pre-packaged ones in supermarket freezers. Admittedly they're
a bit thinner than the norm, but larger and cheaper and they cook
quicker too. With a little imagination you can dish up great tasting
meals using cheaper chops.

Preparation time: 5 mins.   Cooking time: 30 mins.

4 large thin pork chops
Salt and pepper
3 tablsp cooking oil
1 clove garlic, peeled and crushed
2 teasp made English mustard OR mustard powder
¼ pt (150ml) white wine
5 fl oz (150ml) carton soured cream

1.   Season the chops on both sides with salt and pepper.

2.   Heat the oil in a large frying pan and add the garlic and chops.

3.   Fry gently for about 15 minutes on each side until brown and well cooked. Remove the chops to a warm serving dish.

4.   Drain off excess oil leaving the meat sediment in the pan.

5.   Stir in the mustard and then the wine and boil for a couple of minutes.

6.   Remove the pan from the heat and quickly and thoroughly stir in the soured cream. Pour the sauce over the chops.

Serve with green vegetables and new potatoes.

CHINESE GLAZED SPARERIBS   *Serves 4*

When cooked, the ribs are crisp and the sauce thickens to form a lovely sticky glaze. Arm yourself with plenty of paper napkins and eat the ribs with your fingers.

Preparation time: 8 mins.   Cooking time: 50 mins.

2 lb (900g) pork spare ribs
3 tablsp cranberry sauce
2 tablsp tomato ketchup
1 tablsp soy sauce
1 tablsp Worcestershire sauce
2 tablsp clear honey
1 teasp ground ginger
1 teasp mustard
8 oz (225g) can pineapple chunks

1.   Pre-heat the oven to 200°C (400°F) or Gas No 6.

2.   Line a shallow ovenproof dish with foil and arrange the spare ribs on top.

3.   Put all the remaining ingredients in a small pan and heat gently, stirring until smooth.

4. Pour the sauce over the ribs and cook in oven for about 50 minutes. Turn the ribs several times during cooking to make sure all parts are covered with the sauce.

PORK MANDARIN   *Serves 4*

Casseroles take rather longer to cook than other meals, because the cuts of meat are generally cheaper and therefore need longer, slower cooking. However I like those recipes where you throw a few ingredients into a pot and it looks after itself. Use the cooking time to relax with a drink and catch up on the day's gossip with the family.

Preparation time: 10 mins.   Cooking time: 1 hour.

1 lb (450g) belly of pork
1 tablsp cooking oil
1 red pepper, de-seeded and sliced
14 oz (397g) can chopped tomatoes
1 cooking apple, peeled, cored and chopped
½ teasp mixed dried herbs
Salt and pepper
1 tablsp paprika pepper
11 oz (312g) can mandarin oranges, drained

1. Pre-heat oven to 170°C (325°F) or Gas No 3.

2. Trim excess fat off the pork and discard. Cut the flesh into bite-size pieces.

3. Brown the meat in the hot oil, then stir in all the other ingredients except the mandarins.

4. Bring to the boil then transfer to an ovenproof casserole and cook for about an hour until the meat is tender.

5. Stir in the drained mandarins and serve with savoury rice.

CORNED BEEF AND POTATO RISSOLES *Serves 4*

These are a good store cupboard stand-by when children suddenly announce they want a friend to stay for tea. Adults may prefer a tangy sauce accompaniment — just heat up a can of chopped chilli tomatoes.

Preparation time: 15 mins.   Cooking time: 10-16 mins.

4-serving size packet instant potato
1 tablsp Worcestershire sauce
1 tablsp tomato ketchup
Salt and pepper
1 beaten egg
12 oz (340g) can corned beef, cut into small dice

1. Make up the instant potato according to manufacturer's instructions but using a little less water than stated.

2. Stir in Worcestershire sauce, ketchup and seasoning. Set aside to cool slightly.

3. Mix in the beaten egg thoroughly then gently fold in the diced corned beef.

4. Using well floured hands form the mixture into 8 patties.

5. Fry the rissoles in hot shallow oil for about 5 to 8 minutes on each side until brown.

BEAN AND CORNED BEEF HOT POT *Serves 4*

Another favourite with children. You can either use instant mashed potato for the topping, or sliced left-over cold potato.

Preparation time: 15 mins.   Cooking time: 20 mins.

Packet (1½ oz/40g size) beef stew seasoning mix
½ pt (300ml) water
1 onion, peeled and chopped

4-serving packet instant mashed potato
12 oz (340g) can corned beef, cut into cubes
16 oz (450g) can baked beans

1. Pre-heat the oven to 190°C (375°F) or Gas No 5.

2. Place beef seasoning mix, water and onion in a small saucepan. Bring to the boil, stirring all the time, until the gravy thickens. Simmer gently until the onion is tender.

3. Meanwhile, make up the instant potato according to manufacturer's instructions.

4. Stir the cubed corned beef and baked beans into the gravy, turn into an ovenproof dish and allow to cool slightly.

5. Spoon the mashed potato on top, fork up and cook in the oven for about 20 minutes until potato is nicely browned. (Brushing the potato with a little beaten egg before cooking will assist browning.) Serve with green vegetables.

STEAK DIANE   *Serves 2*

This is rich, luxurious and expensive — but quick! If money is no object try it for a romantic dinner *à deux!*

Preparation time: 8 mins.   Cooking time: 10-20 mins.

2 fillet steaks (allow about 6 oz (175g) per person)
Salt
Knob butter
1 onion, peeled and chopped finely
1 tablsp black peppercorns, crushed
1 teasp Worcestershire sauce
1 tablsp lemon juice
1 tablsp brandy
4 tablsp double cream

1. Season the steak with salt. Melt the butter in a frying pan and
    add the onion and crushed peppercorns. Fry gently for about
    5 minutes.

2. Add the steaks and fry for 5-10 minutes on each side,
    depending on whether they are to be rare, medium or well
    done.

    Push the meat to one side and stir in the Worcestershire sauce,
    lemon juice, brandy and cream. Heat gently but do not boil.
    Garnish with chopped fresh parsley if liked.

An equally delicious variation on the above recipe can be made
by omitting the Worcestershire sauce, lemon juice and brandy and
adding 3 tablespoons of Drambuie instead. Simmer the liqueur
for a few minutes to reduce slightly then stir in the cream.

LIVER WITH PEPPERCORN SAUCE   *Serves 4*

From the sublime to the ridiculous! Liver is a rich form of iron
although many people, including children, aren't keen. However
it is cheap and offers good value because there is no waste. Try
disguising the liver with this delicious sauce!
    Calf's liver is the best; tender and delicate in flavour. Lamb's
liver, although a little cheaper has a stronger flavour. Ox and pig's
liver have a very pronounced flavour and are best avoided if you
are trying to woo the family.

Preparation time: 5 mins.   Cooking time: 10 mins.

1 tablsp cooking oil
Knob butter or margarine
1 lb (450g) liver, sliced thinly
Salt and pepper
1 tablsp green peppercorns in brine, chopped
½ beef stock cube, made up with ¼ pt (150ml) water
5 fl oz (150ml) carton soured cream

1. Heat the oil with the butter or margarine in a frying pan.

2. Add the seasoned liver and chopped peppercorns and fry gently for about 10 minutes until the meat is cooked. Remove and keep warm.

3. Add the stock to the pan juices and simmer until it has reduced and thickened slightly.

4. Stir in the soured cream and heat to just below boiling. Pour over the liver and garnish with chopped parsley if liked.

KIDNEYS À L'ORANGE   *Serves 4*

Again this recipe has a nice flavour to tempt those who turn their noses up at kidneys.

Preparation time: 15 mins.   Cooking time: 20 mins.

**8-12 lamb's kidneys, skinned, halved and cored
2 tablsp flour
Salt and pepper
½ teasp cayenne pepper
1 onion, peeled and sliced
1 tablsp cooking oil
½ beef stock cube made up with ¼ pt (150ml) water
7 oz (200g) can tomatoes
Grated rind and juice of 1 orange**

1. Put the prepared kidneys, flour, salt, pepper and cayenne in a small polythene bag. Toss around to make sure the kidneys are well coated.

2. Fry the onion with the kidneys in the oil until brown on both sides.

3. Stir in any remaining flour together with the stock, tomatoes, orange rind and juice. Cover and cook gently for about 20 minutes. Serve garnished with triangles of fried bread.

HONEY AND MUSTARD GLAZED LAMB *Serves 4*

Nothing could be easier and quicker to prepare than this honey
and mustard glaze which imparts a delicious flavour to lamb. (For
a single serving, use one lamb chop and a glaze made with half
a teaspoon of honey and half a teaspoon of French mustard.)

Preparation time: 4 mins.   Cooking time: 30 mins.

4 boneless lamb chump chops
2 tablsp clear honey
2 teasp French mustard

1.   Pre-heat oven to 200°C (400°F) or Gas No 6.

2.   Place the chops on a sheet of foil.

3.   Mix the honey and mustard together and spoon over the chops.
     Secure the foil in a parcel.

4.   Cook for 15 minutes then open up the foil and cook for a
     further 15 minutes.

MEAT BALLS IN TOMATO SOUP   *Serves 4*

This quick and easy dish is a great favourite with children and is
good served with noodles or rice.

Preparation time: 10 mins.   Cooking time: 25 mins.

12 oz (350g) minced beef
Salt and pepper
1 onion, peeled and finely chopped
1 egg, beaten
Flour
15 oz (425g) can cream of tomato soup

1.   Bind the mince, seasoning, onion and egg well together, using
     your hand if necessary.

2. Flour your hands and form the mixture into about 14 balls. Roll each in flour.

3. Heat the soup to simmering point in a saucepan and add the meat balls. Cook gently for about 25 minutes, turning once during cooking.

CIDER BAKED SAUSAGES

Serves 4

Use good quality butcher's sausages for this recipe — nice and herby and spicy — not those mealy, tasteless supermarket jobs! Serve with scrubbed new potatoes and a watercress and orange salad.

Preparation time: 8 mins.   Cooking time: 40 mins.

1 lb (450g) sausages
3 sharp eating apples
1 onion, peeled and sliced
½ pt (500ml) medium sweet cider

1. Pre-heat oven to 200°C (400°F) or Gas No 6.

2. Prick the sausages and place them in an ovenproof dish.

3. Quarter, peel and core the apples and cut the flesh into slices. Put the apples and onion slices in between the sausages and pour over the cider.

4. Bake in oven for about 40 minutes, turning the sausages, and stirring the apple and onion mixture, halfway through cooking.

N.B. Cooking time is based on thick sausages, thin ones will cook quicker. At the end, the cider and apples should have reduced to form a syrupy and fruity sauce.

ORANGE GLAZED PORK WITH VEGETABLES
Serves 4

An orange and honey marinade is brushed on the pork before cooking and also tossed through hot vegetables as a dressing. Small new potatoes or special salad potatoes, which are available at large supermarkets, are particularly good for this dish.

Preparation time: 10 mins.   Cooking time: 20 mins.

8 oz (225g) salad potatoes OR small new potatoes
8 oz (225g) dwarf green beans
1 lb (450g) pork tenderloin
2 tablsp cooking oil
Salt and pepper
Juice 1 orange
1 teasp clear honey
4 tomatoes, quartered

1.   Cook the potatoes in boiling salted water until tender, about 20 minutes. Drain.

2.   Take the bunch of dwarf beans and cut the stalks off in one go. Cook in boiling salted water until just tender, about 10 minutes.

3.   Cut the pork into ½" (1.5cm) slices and place in a grill pan. (By lining the pan with foil first, there will be no tedious washing up!)

4.   Mix the oil, seasoning, orange juice and honey together and brush the liquid liberally over the pork. Cook under a medium grill for about 8 minutes on each side, brushing frequently with the marinade.

5.   Add the tomato quarters to the potatoes and beans and gently toss in the remaining marinade.

MEXICAN TACOS   *Serves 4*

These are very tasty, but economical because a little meat goes
a long way. Serve with savoury rice and/or red kidney beans.

Preparation time: 8 mins.   Cooking time: 20 mins.

1 onion, peeled and chopped
1 clove garlic, peeled and finely chopped
12 oz (350g) minced beef
1 tablsp cooking oil
2 teasp Mexican chilli seasoning
10.6 oz (300g) can condensed tomato rice soup
2 tablsp water
Salt and pepper
8 taco shells
5 fl oz (150ml) carton soured cream }   **for garnish**
Shredded lettuce   **(optional)**

1. Pre-heat oven to 180°C (350°F) or Gas No 4.

2. Fry the onion, garlic and minced beef in the oil for about 10
    minutes, breaking the meat up with a fork.

3. Stir in the Mexican seasoning, soup and water and simmer
    over a low heat for a further 10 minutes, stirring occasionally.
    Season to taste.

4. Meanwhile heat the taco shells in the oven for a couple of
    minutes.

5. Fill the tacos with the meat mixture, top with a spoonful of
    soured cream and garnish with shredded lettuce.

LAMB SEVILLE   *Serves 4*

180ml bottles of tomato juice cocktail are available from most
supermarkets. Use these to save time; they include Worcestershire
sauce so you can omit it from the recipe. Serve with small new
potatoes and salad.

Preparation time: 8 mins.   Cooking time: 40 mins.

4 boneless lamb chump chops or steaks
1 green pepper, de-seeded and cut into chunks
1 onion, peeled and sliced
1 heaped teasp flour
Salt and pepper
2 tablsp orange marmalade
1 teasp Worcestershire sauce
Juice 1 orange
6 fl oz (180ml) tomato juice

1.   Pre-heat oven to 190°C (375°F) or Gas No 5.

2.   Put chops, pepper and onion in an ovenproof dish.

3.   Put the flour, seasoning and marmalade in a small bowl and gradually stir in the Worcestershire sauce, orange juice and tomato juice.

4.   Pour the mixture over the chops, cover with a lid or foil and bake for about 40 minutes, until the meat is tender. (Halfway through cooking turn the chops over; and remove lid or foil for the last 10 minutes.)

PORK STROGANOFF   *Serves 4*

This is a delicious recipe which would do justice to a dinner party, and it won't keep you in the kitchen all night or spoil if guests are late. Serve with brown rice and lightly cooked courgettes.

Preparation time: 10 mins.   Cooking time: 25 mins.

1 onion, peeled and chopped
6 oz (175g) mushrooms, sliced
1 tablsp cooking oil
1 lb (450g) pork tenderloin, thinly sliced
1 tablsp flour
Salt and pepper

2 tablsp tomato purée
1 stock cube, made up with 7 fl oz (200ml) water
5 fl oz (150ml) carton soured cream
Chopped parsley for garnish (optional)

1. Fry the onion and mushrooms gently in the oil for 10 minutes.

2. Push the vegetables to the side, add the pork and cook for 5
    minutes until brown on all sides.

3. Remove from heat and stir in the flour, seasoning, tomato
    purée and stock. Simmer gently for about 10 minutes until
    the meat is cooked. Stir occasionally.

4. Stir in the soured cream and serve garnished with chopped
    parsley if liked.

SPICY MEAT VOL-AU-VENTS   *Serves 4*

Pastry adds bulk to a meal thus making economical use of meat.
Serve these mildly spiced vol-au-vents with small new potatoes
and carrots.

Preparation time: 5 mins.   Cooking time: 25 mins.

4 king-size vol-au-vents
1 onion, peeled and chopped
1 small green pepper, de-seeded and diced
1 tablsp cooking oil
8 oz (225g) minced beef
1 tablsp curry paste
Packet (1½ oz/40g size) beef seasoning mix
8 fl oz (250ml) water

1. Pre-heat oven to 220°C (425°F) or Gas No 7 and cook the
    vol-au-vents for about 12 minutes until well risen and light
    brown.

2. Fry the onion and pepper in the oil for about 10 minutes.

3. Add mince, breaking it up with a fork, and brown for about 5 minutes.

4. Stir in the curry paste, beef seasoning mix and water. Simmer gently, stirring until the mixture thickens.

5. Remove the lids from the vol-au-vents and pull out and discard the uncooked pastry.

6. Pile the meat mixture into the vol-au-vents and pop on the lids.

GRILLED LIVER WITH CITRUS SAUCE   *Serves 4*

Liver cooks in minutes but accompanied by this delicious tangy sauce it is designed to be savoured much longer.

Preparation time: 5 mins.   Cooking time: 12 mins.

1 tablsp sugar
2 tablsp wine vinegar
Juice ½ lemon
Juice 1 orange
1 stock cube made up with 8 fl oz (225ml) water
1 onion, peeled and chopped
1 lb (450g) calf's liver, thinly sliced
Wedges fresh lime for garnish (optional)
Chopped fresh sage for garnish (optional)

1. Put the sugar and vinegar in a small saucepan and cook over a low heat until the sugar has dissolved.

2. Boil rapidly until mixture begins to caramelise.

3. Add lemon juice, orange juice, stock and onion and boil until the liquid has reduced by half.

4. Meanwhile grill the liver for a few minutes on each side so that the inside remains creamy in texture and pale pink in colour.

5. Arrange the liver on serving plates and pour over the fruity sauce. If liked, garnish with lime and chopped sage.

COLE'S KIDNEYS

Serves 4

Named after the friend who donated this tasty recipe which he often
cooks for quickness after a hard day's work! Serve with rice and
croûtons of fried bread.

Preparation time: 8 mins. Cooking time: 20 mins.

10-12 lamb's kidneys
Knob butter or margarine
1 tablsp cooking oil
1 onion, peeled and chopped
4 oz (100g) mushrooms, sliced
1 tablsp flour
Salt and pepper
1 stock cube, made up with scant ½ pt (300ml) water
2 tablsp sherry

1. Remove skin, then slice the kidneys horizontally. Using
    scissors, cut out the white core and as many tubes as possible.

2. Heat the butter or margarine and the oil in a frying pan.

3. Sauté the kidneys, onion and mushrooms for about 5 minutes
    until the meat has browned.

4. Stir in the flour, seasoning, stock and sherry. Simmer gently
    for 15 minutes, stirring occasionally.

9 POULTRY

Chicken and turkey are good sources of protein, contain little fat and offer good value for money. Larger chicken joints which contain a bone don't shallow fry very well because of their uneven thickness and non-uniform shape. It is essential that chicken is cooked thoroughly; test by piercing with a skewer — the juices that run out should be clear. Such joints are better cooked in a medium oven for about 45 minutes. Thin turkey escallops are also well worth buying.

Cuts containing a bone are cheaper, and although you can use them in the following recipes, cooking times will need to be extended. Chicken can be combined with an infinite variety of ingredients to make interesting meals and offers endless possibilities for experimenting with different flavours.

QUICK CORONATION CHICKEN
Serves 4

This is a quick version of the classic recipe made for the Queen's coronation in 1953. The dish improves if made the day before eating which makes it an ideal lunch if guests are staying. No spending hours in the kitchen when you could be enjoying the cameraderie! Either buy a whole cooked chicken, or if time permits cook your own in a large saucepan of water to which salt,

pepper, bay leaf and a few chunks of raw onion have been added.
A 3 lb (1.35k) chicken yields about 1 lb (450g) flesh.

Preparation time: 15-20 mins.   Cooking time: None.

1 lb (450g) cooked chicken, cut into strips
2 tablsp toasted flaked almonds
1 tablsp sultanas
4 tablsp mayonnaise
5 fl oz (150 ml) Greek yoghurt
2 teasp curry paste
1 teasp soft brown sugar
2 sticks celery, thinly sliced

Combine all the ingredients and mix well. Garnish with
watercress and different varieties of lettuce.

CHICKEN À L'ORANGE
Serves 4

Garlicy orange butter renders the chicken moist and flavourful.
Serve with wild rice and mixed salad. Depending on appetite,
allow 2-3 chicken thighs per person.

Preparation time: 8 mins.   Cooking time: 25 mins.

8-12 boneless and skinless chicken thighs
1 tablsp butter or margarine
2 cloves garlic, peeled and finely chopped
1 tablsp flour
1 teasp soft brown sugar
Salt and pepper
Grated rind and juice of 1 orange

1. Pre-heat oven to 200°C (400°F) or Gas No 6.

2. Using a sharp knife, score each chicken piece with three deep
    cuts.

3. In a small bowl combine the butter or margarine, garlic, flour,
    sugar, seasoning, orange rind and one tablespoon of juice.

4. Using a round-bladed knife fill the cuts in the chicken with
    the butter mixture.

5.   Place the chicken close together in a shallow ovenproof dish
     and pour over the remaining orange juice. Cook for about 25
     minutes.

MEXICAN HONEYED CHICKEN   *Serves 4*

When cooked, the honey crisps to a sticky glaze, its sweetness
offset by the chilli powder. (For a single serving, use two or three
chicken thighs and make the glaze with 1 tablespoon of honey and
half a teaspoon of chilli powder.)

Preparation time: 5 mins.   Cooking time: 25 mins.

8-12 boneless and skinless chicken thighs
4 tablsp clear honey
2 teasp chilli powder
Salt and pepper

1.   Pre-heat oven to 200°C (400°F) or Gas No 6.

2.   Using a sharp knife, score each chicken piece with three deep
     cuts.

3.   In a small bowl blend the honey, chilli powder, salt and pepper.

4.   Place the chicken close together in a shallow ovenproof dish.
     Spoon the honey mixture into the cuts.

5.   Bake in the oven for about 25 minutes.

TURKEY CAPPARIS   *Serves 4*

Named after the caper, a bramble-like Mediterranean shrub,
whose flower buds are pickled for culinary use. You could use
green peppercorns in brine instead of capers — either one imparts
a sharp bite to the bland creamy sauce. (See page 23 for serving
one or two.)

Preparation time: 5 mins.   Cooking time: 20 mins.

Knob butter or margarine
1 tablsp cooking oil
2 tablsp capers or green peppercorns in brine
Salt and pepper
4 turkey escallops
1 teasp flour
¼ pt (150ml) white grape juice
2 tablsp double cream

1. Heat the butter or margarine with the oil in a large frying pan
    and toss in the capers or peppercorns.

2. Season the turkey and brown quickly on both sides.

3. Stir in the flour to the pan juices and pour in the grape juice.

4. Simmer gently until the turkey is cooked, about 8 minutes
    each side. The liquid should have thickened, if it hasn't
    continue cooking for a further few minutes.

5. Stir in the cream and adjust seasoning if necessary.

CHICKEN TERYAKI   *Serves 4*

The sauce cooks to a syrupy glaze which nicely complements the
delicate flavour of chicken.

Preparation time: 5 mins.   Cooking time: 20 mins.

Knob butter or margarine
1 tablsp cooking oil
2 teasp sesame seeds
3-4 boneless and skinless chicken breasts
1 teasp soft brown sugar
1 tablsp clear honey
2 tablsp soy sauce
Juice 1 lemon
Knob fresh ginger, peeled and coarsely grated

1. Heat the butter or margarine with the oil in a large frying pan,
    add the sesame seeds and fry for a few seconds until brown.

2. Cut the chicken into diagonal slices. Add to the pan and brown quickly on both sides.

3. Stir in the sugar, honey, soy sauce, lemon juice and ginger.

4. Simmer for about 15-20 minutes, turning the chicken occasionally. The liquid should be syrupy. Serve with pillau rice and a watercress and orange salad.

TANDOORI CHICKEN   *Serves 4*

This mildly spiced dish is a perennial favourite. The chicken should be brown and crusty on the outside and moist inside. Naan bread and a mixed salad make ideal accompaniments. (See page 23 for serving one or two.)

Preparation time: 5 mins.   Cooking time: 30 mins.

8-12 boneless and skinless chicken thighs
5 fl oz (150ml) Greek yoghurt
Juice 1 lemon
2 cloves garlic, peeled and very finely chopped
1 teasp garam masala
1 teasp paprika
1 teasp turmeric
2 teasp ground coriander
Salt and pepper
Chopped fresh coriander for garnish (optional)

1. Pre-heat oven to 200°C (400°F) or Gas No 6.

2. Make several deep cuts in the chicken pieces.

3. Combine all the remaining ingredients except the fresh coriander.

4. Put the chicken in a shallow ovenproof dish and spoon over the marinade, rubbing it well into the cuts.

5. Bake for 30 minutes until the chicken is tender and garnish with chopped coriander if liked.

LEMON FRIED CHICKEN *Serves 4*

Slivers of chicken are deep fried in a lemon crumb coating. Serve with a mayonnaise-based dip.

Preparation time: 12 mins.   Cooking time: 8 mins.

8 boneless and skinless chicken thighs
1 egg, beaten
1 tablsp self-raising flour
5 tablsp commercially prepared breadcrumbs
1 teasp turmeric
2 teasp ground coriander
Salt and pepper
Finely grated rind 1 lemon

1. Cut the chicken into thin strips.

2. Toss the chicken in the beaten egg.

3. Put the flour, breadcrumbs, turmeric, coriander, seasoning and lemon rind in a small polythene bag. Add the chicken in two or three batches and shake the bag until the chicken is well coated with the mix.

4. Fry in deep hot oil for about 8 minutes until golden brown and cooked through. Drain on kitchen paper.

5. Serve squeezed with lemon juice, using the lemon from which the rind was grated.

CURRIED HAWAIIAN TURKEY *Serves 4*

This is a simple no-hassle dish to prepare. The combination of curry powder and pineapple complements turkey or chicken particularly well. It is not at all hot and spicy and I find the flavour appeals to children.

Preparation time: 6 mins.   Cooking time: 25 mins.

2 tablsp cooking oil
1 onion, peeled and chopped
Salt and pepper
4 turkey escallops
1 tablsp flour
2 tablsp mild curry powder
1 stock cube, made up with 7 fl oz (200ml) water
15 oz (400g) can crushed pineapple

1. Heat the oil in a large frying pan and add the onion.

2. Season the turkey escallops and place them on top of the
    onion. Fry gently for five minutes on each side.

3. Mix the flour and curry powder together, sprinkle over the
    escallops and turn them over.

4. Add stock and crushed pineapple with juice.

5. Simmer for about 15 minutes turning the escallops over once.
    If the sauce becomes too thick during cooking, add a dash of
    water.

DEVILLED CHICKEN DRUMSTICKS   *Serves 4*

This tasty oily marinade is ideal for using on meat which is to be
barbequed. Serve the drumsticks with salad and garlic bread. (For
a single serving use about two drumsticks and make up the
marinade with 1 tablespoon of oil, a shake of paprika and ginger
and half a teaspoon of mustard powder. If, when you come to make
the dish again, a more distinctive flavour is preferred, simply add
more of the spices.)

Preparation time: 5 mins.   Cooking time: 40 mins.

8 chicken drumsticks
4 fl oz (100ml) cooking oil
Salt and pepper
1 teasp paprika
1 teasp powdered ginger
2 teasp mustard powder

1. Pre-heat oven to 200°C (400°F) or Gas No 6.

2. Using a sharp knife make three or four slashes in each drumstick and place them close together in a shallow ovenproof dish.

3. Combine the remaining ingredients in a small screw top jar and shake until well mixed.

4. Pour the liquid over the chicken and cook for about 40 minutes, basting frequently.

CHICKEN AND HAM VOL-AU-VENTS   *Serves 4*

Condensed soups make instant sauces and can be combined with left-over meat and vegetables for tasty pastry fillings.

Preparation time: 8 mins.   Cooking time: 17 mins.

4 king-size vol-au-vents
Handful of frozen peas
4 oz (100g) cooked chicken, diced
4 oz (100g) cooked ham, diced
Freshly ground black pepper
10.4 oz (295g) can condensed chicken soup

1. Pre-heat oven to 220°C (425°F) or Gas No 7 and cook the vol-au-vents for about 12 minutes until well risen and light brown.

2. Put the peas in a bowl, pour on boiling water and leave until the vol-au-vents are cooked, then drain.

3. Mix the chicken, ham, black pepper, soup and drained peas together.

4. Remove the lids from the vol-au-vents and pull out uncooked pastry and discard.

5. Fill the vol-au-vents with the chicken mixture, pop on the pastry lids and heat in the oven for about 5 minutes.

10 TELEVISION SUPPERS, SNACKS AND SALADS

This chapter aims for the bistro or wine-bar-style snack, ideal for days when you don't feel like a hearty meal.

For instance there are times when all families like to huddle round the fire, watching a favourite television programme, with a fork in one hand and something tasty to eat in the other.

In summer something light and cool is welcome, an all-in-one-salad perhaps, which can be served with chunks of fresh bread and butter and enjoyed in the garden.

STUFFED PÂTÉ MUSHROOMS   *Serves 4*

These are rich and delicious; hot garlic bread and a salad of shredded lettuce, watercress, cucumber and tomato make good accompaniments. A vegetarian stuffing could be made by using mushroom pâté.

Preparation time: 15 mins.   Cooking time: 10 mins.

8 large flat mushrooms
Cooking oil
6 oz (175g) good quality smooth pâté
2 tablsp medium sherry
Juice 1 lemon
4 tablsp herb and garlic stuffing mix
1 teasp chopped fresh rosemary (optional)

1. Pre-heat oven to 200°C (400°F) or Gas No 6.

2. Remove mushroom stalks and reserve. Put the caps in a roasting tin and pour in enough oil to cover the base. Brush mushrooms liberally with the oil.

3. Mix pâté, sherry, lemon juice, stuffing mix and rosemary well together. Spoon the mixture on to the mushrooms and replace the stalks.

4. Brush again with oil, bake in the oven for 10 minutes and serve immediately.

HOT CREAM CHEESE WITH PRAWNS *Serves 4*

This recipe was cadged from my local wine bar! You can eat it like pâté on melba toast, crackers or chunks of fresh bread. Serve with a salad garnish of celery and carrot sticks.

Preparation time: 5 mins.   *Cooking time: 3 mins.*

14 oz (400g) cream cheese
1 tablsp French mustard
2 spring onions, chopped
4 oz (100g) peeled prawns
Grated Parmesan cheese

1. Pre-heat oven to 220°C (425°F) or Gas No 7.

2. Mix the cream cheese, mustard, spring onions and prawns well together and press into 4 individual ovenproof dishes,

sprinkle liberally with grated Parmesan and pop in the oven
for a few minutes.

SUMMER BEEF SALAD   *Serves 4*

This is a good way of using up cold beef from a roast joint.
Alternatively you can buy cold sliced beef from a delicatessen or
supermarket. The parsley is an essential ingredient to the flavour
so use it if you can. Serve with fresh crusty bread.

Preparation time: 15 mins.   Cooking time: None.

12 oz (350g) cold roast beef
1 eating apple, peeled, cored and diced
½ cucumber, peeled and diced
2 celery sticks, sliced
1 bunch parsley, chopped
2 tablsp olive oil
Juice 1 lemon
1 tablsp soy sauce

1.   Cut the beef into strips and mix with the apple, cucumber,
     celery and parsley.

2.   Mix the oil, lemon juice and soy sauce together. (A screw-
     top jar is ideal for making liquid dressings as all the ingredients
     can be shaken well together.)

3.   Fold the dressing through the beef mixture and turn into a
     serving dish.

POTTED SHRIMPS   *Serves 4*

These make a tasty light snack or a quick starter for a dinner party.
Serve with thin slices of toast. Allow 30 minutes chilling time
before eating.

Preparation time: 3 mins.   Cooking time: 5 mins.

7 oz (200g) can shrimps, drained
3 oz (75g) butter
1 teasp paprika
Dash cayenne (optional)
Freshly ground black pepper
Wedges of lemon and salad greens for garnish

1. Heat the shrimps and butter together in a small saucepan for a few minutes.

2. Stir in the paprika, cayenne (if using) and black pepper and cook gently for a couple of minutes.

3. Press the mixture into 4 individual pots and chill for about 30 minutes until solidified.

4. Turn out on to small plates and garnish with wedges of lemon and salad greens.

AVOCADO WITH SPICY TUNA   *Serves 4*

The piquant tuna mixture goes really well with the bland flavour of avocados. Serve with garlic bread and a green salad.

Preparation time: 15 mins.   Cooking time: None.

7 oz (200g) can tuna fish, drained
3 tablsp mayonnaise
3 teasp Worcestershire sauce
2 teasp tomato purée
Juice ½ lemon
1 small onion, peeled and finely chopped
Salt and black pepper
4 avocado pears

1. Roughly flake the tuna into a bowl and add all the ingredients except the pears.

2. Halve and peel the avocados and discard the stones. Slice the

pears so that the halves fan out on the plate. Pile the tuna mixture in the centre and sprinkle with a little cayenne pepper if liked. Garnish with shredded lettuce.

AVOCADO AND BACON SALAD   *Serves 4*

Another tasty avocado salad. Use a dressing of your choice — mild curry, thousand island, blue cheese or herb and garlic are all good. Alternatively soured cream and chopped chives go well with bacon.

Preparation time: 10 mins.   Cooking time: 15 mins.

12 oz (350g) smoked streaky bacon, diced
4 avocados
Mixed salad
4 generous tablsp mayonnaise-based dressing

1. Fry the diced bacon until crisp, about 15 minutes.

2. Meanwhile, halve, peel and de-stone the avocados. Avocado flesh discolours when exposed to the air. If you are preparing this dish more than about 40 minutes before eating, it is advisable to brush lemon juice on the cut edges.

3. Arrange a salad on 4 individual plates and place the avocados on top, cut side down.

4. Spoon the dressing over the avocados and top with crispy bacon.

PRAWN AND SWEETCORN TOAST TOPPER
Serves 4

For a 'hot' version add a good shake of cayenne pepper to the mixture. Serve with thin slices of toast and a salad garnish.

Preparation time: 10 mins.   Cooking time: 15 mins.

2 eggs, hardboiled
Packet (standard/17g size) white sauce mix (makes ½ pint)
7 fl oz (200ml) milk
4 oz (100g) peeled prawns
7 oz (200g) can sweetcorn, drained
4 oz (100g) mature Cheddar cheese, grated

1. While the eggs are boiling, make up the sauce mix according to manufacturer's instructions but only use 7 fl oz (200ml) milk.

2. Stir in the prawns, sweetcorn and three quarters of the cheese.

3. Peel and chop the eggs and stir into the sauce. Spoon the mixture into 4 heatproof dishes, top with remaining cheese and brown under a hot grill for about 5 minutes.

Grilled or fried sandwiches make tasty quick snacks which satisfy the heartiest appetite. Sliced bread, pittas, halved rolls or split French sticks are suitable for a variety of fillings or toppings. I'm sure you can create your own combinations but here are a few ideas to start you off. Snacks like these are good during the school holidays — older children could even make their own.

CROQUE MONSIEUR   *Serves 4*

Just about any cheese is suitable, from processed cheese slices to Mozzarella. I particularly like the latter because it goes deliciously gooey and stringy when cooked.

Preparation time: 10 mins.   Cooking time: 8 mins.

Butter or margarine
8 slices medium sliced bread
4 slices cooked ham
Slices of cheese — Cheddar, Gruyère or Mozzarella

1. Butter each slice of bread on one side only.

2.   With butter side out, sandwich together in pairs with a slice
     of ham and some cheese.

3.   Grill gently for about 4 minutes on each side until the cheese
     has melted and the bread is golden brown.

EGG AND BACON TOASTIES   *Serves 4*

Preparation time: 10 mins.   Cooking time: 15 mins.

6 rashers smoked streaky bacon, diced
3 eggs
2 tablsp mayonnaise
Salt and pepper
4-6 slices buttered toast
Slices of tomato (optional)

1.   Grill or fry the diced bacon until crisp.

2.   Hardboil the eggs then peel and chop.

3.   Mix the bacon, eggs, mayonnaise and seasoning together and
     spread on buttered toast.

4.   Top with slices of tomato, if liked, and pop under a hot grill
     for a minute to brown. Cut into triangles.

CHEESE AND PINEAPPLE TOASTIES   *Serves 4*

Preparation time: 10 mins.   Cooking time: 5 mins.

4 slices cooked ham, diced
4 oz (100g) mature Cheddar cheese, grated
2 tablsp canned crushed pineapple
4-6 slices buttered toast

1.   Mix the ham, cheese and pineapple together. Spread the
     mixture on buttered toast and pop under a medium grill until
     golden and bubbly.

SAVOURY PITTAS
Serves 4

Pitta bread makes a good base for all types of tasty toppings. Use left-overs or bits and pieces from the store cupboard and top with slices of cheese.

Preparation time: 10 mins.   Cooking time: 5 mins.

Handful of dried sliced mushrooms
4 individual pittas
2 sun-dried tomatoes OR ½-1 tablsp tomato purée
8 slices salami
Slices Mozzarella cheese

1. Put the mushrooms in a cup and pour on boiling water. Leave for 10 minutes.

2. Smear the pitta bread with sun-dried tomatoes or tomato purée.

3. Top with salami, the drained mushrooms and cheese.

4. Pop under a medium grill for about 5 minutes until the cheese is gooey.

TOASTED CHEESE AND TUNA ROLLS   *Serves 4*

Preparation time: 10 mins.   Cooking time: 5 mins.

4 baps
7 oz (200g) can tuna fish, drained
7 oz (200g) can sweetcorn, drained
3 tablsp mayonnaise
2 oz (50g) mature Cheddar cheese, grated

1. Split the baps in half.

2. Mix the tuna, corn, mayonnaise and cheese together. Pile the mixture on the rolls and grill for about 5 minutes.

BAKED BRIE WITH APPLES AND ALMONDS

Serves 4

A new angle on plain old cheese and biscuits. This is another wine-bar recipe and is lovely served with buttered crackers or chunks of wholemeal bread.

Preparation time: 5 mins.   Cooking time: 4 mins.

4 pieces fresh Brie
2 tablsp flaked almonds
2 sharp eating apples, quartered, cored and sliced

1. Pre-heat oven to 220°C (425°F) or Gas No 7.

2. Put the pieces of Brie on four individual ovenproof plates and sprinkle some nuts over each.

3. Pop into the oven for about 4 minutes until the cheese has slightly melted and the nuts browned.

4. Arrange the sliced apples down one side of the cheese and the crackers or bread on the other.

ITALIAN SALAD

Serves 4

For a more substantial meal, add a few rolled up anchovies and some sliced salami. Serve with one of the more unusual varieties of lettuce like Lollo Rosso, Quattro Stagioni or Radicchio (a red leafed Italian chicory). All are usually available from larger supermarkets. Hot garlic bread is also a delicious accompaniment.

Preparation time: 15 mins.   Cooking time: None.

1 lb (450g) beefsteak tomatoes
4 oz (100g) Mozzarella cheese
1 small onion
7 oz (200g) can sweet red peppers, drained

Few black olives, stoned
2 teasp chopped fresh basil OR 1 teasp dried
4 tablsp olive oil
Juice 1 lemon
1 tablsp white wine vinegar
Pinch sugar
Salt and pepper

1. Slice the tomatoes and cheese and arrange in a shallow dish.

2. Peel and cut the onion into wafer thin slices.

3. Cut the peppers into strips.

4. Arrange the onion, peppers and olives on top of the cheese and tomatoes.

5. Put the basil, oil, lemon juice, vinegar, sugar and seasoning into a screw-top jar and shake well until thick. Pour the dressing over the salad.

WALDORF SALAD WITH PEACHES   *Serves 4*

This is a variation on a classic salad using fresh peaches as well as apples. Served on its own it makes an ideal light summer supper, but for a more substantial meal accompany with fresh bread and a selection of cheese.

Preparation time: 20 mins.   Cooking time: 5 mins.

8 oz (225g) dwarf green beans
1 red eating apple
1 green eating apple
2 fresh peaches
1 stick celery
2 oz (50g) walnut pieces
5 oz (150g) carton natural yoghurt
2 tablsp mayonnaise
Juice 1 orange

1. Cook the beans in boiling salted water for about 5 minutes, until just tender. Drain.

2. Quarter the apples, remove cores and slice the flesh into a bowl.

3. Halve the peaches, remove stones and slice the flesh into the bowl.

4. Thinly slice the celery and add to the bowl together with the walnuts and drained beans.

5. Combine the yoghurt, mayonnaise and orange juice and fold through the fruit and vegetable mixture.

PRAWN COCKTAIL VOL-AU-VENTS   *Serves 4*

These make a tasty quick summer supper. Serve with mixed salad and some sliced chicory tossed in vinaigrette dressing.

Preparation time: 8 mins.   Cooking time: 12 mins.

4 king-size frozen vol-au-vents
8 oz (225g) peeled prawns
2 tablsp tomato purée or ketchup
4 tablsp mayonnaise
Ground black pepper
Shredded lettuce
Lemon wedges for garnish (optional)

1. Pre-heat oven to 200°C (425°F) or Gas No 7. Cook the vol-au-vents for about 12 minutes until well risen and lightly brown. Allow to cool slightly.

2. Meanwhile mix the prawns, tomato purée or ketchup, mayonnaise and black pepper together.

3. Remove the lids from the vol-au-vents and pull out uncooked pastry and discard.

4. Half fill the vol-au-vents with shredded lettuce then fill with
    the prawn mixture and pop back the pastry lids. Garnish with
    lemon wedges if liked.

HOT PITTA POCKETS

If you slit open pitta bread it forms a natural pocket which can be
stuffed with a variety of tasty fillings. No doubt you will devise
your own combinations but here are two delicious recipes to give
you an idea. Quantities given are enough for 6-8 mini, or 4-6 large
pittas, depending on how much filling you want to put in. The
stuffed pittas are wrapped in foil and cooked in a hot oven for a
few minutes. Serve with a selection of raw vegetables — carrot
and celery sticks, chunks of tomato and cucumber and chicory
leaves are all ideal.

MEXICAN PITTAS   *Serves 4*

Preparation time: 8 mins.   Cooking time: 7 mins.

Pitta bread
8 oz (225g) sliced salami
15 oz (425g) can red kidney beans, drained
6 tablsp garlic mayonnaise
Few drops Tabasco sauce (optional)

1. Pre-heat oven to 200°C (400°F) or Gas No 6.

2. Split the pitta bread to form a pocket and line with slices of
    salami.

3. Mix the beans, mayonnaise and Tabasco sauce together and
    spoon into the pitta bread.

4. Wrap each individually in foil and bake for about 7 minutes.

CREAM CHEESE AND BACON PITTAS   *Serves 4*

Preparation time: 8 mins.   Cooking time: 17 mins.

6 oz (175g) smoked streaky bacon
8 oz (225g) cream cheese
1 tomato, chopped
Freshly ground black pepper
Few chopped chives (optional)
Pitta bread

1. Pre-heat the oven to 200°C (400°F) or Gas No 6.

2. Grill the bacon until crisp, about 10 minutes, then roughly chop it.

3. Mix the bacon, cream cheese, tomato, pepper and chives together.

4. Split the pitta bread to form a pocket and stuff with the cheese mixture.

5. Wrap each individually in foil and bake for about 7 minutes.

SAVOURY CHOUX BUNS   *Makes 4*

Contrary to popular belief, choux pastry is quick and easy and makes a useful base for savoury and sweet dishes. (See also chapter on Desssèrts.) Choux buns are airy in texture, just the thing for a luxury filling of cream cheese and smoked salmon. Look for the packets of trimmings which are much cheaper than prime slices.

Preparation time: 10 mins.   Cooking time: 30 mins.

2 oz (50g) butter or margarine
¼ pt (150ml) water
2½ oz (65g) plain flour
Pinch salt
2 eggs, beaten

Filling
Smoked salmon trimmings
Cream cheese
Slices cucumber
Slices chicory

1. Pre-heat oven to 220°C (425°F) or Gas No 7.

2. Melt the butter or margarine in a small saucepan, add the water and bring to the boil.

3. Stir in the flour and salt all at once and beat over a low heat until the mixture leaves the side of the pan. Allow to cool for a minute or two.

4. Gradually add the eggs, beating well between each addition until the pastry is smooth.

5. Spoon four heaps of the choux pastry on to a damp baking tray and cook for 10 minutes. Turn oven down to 190°C (375°F) or Gas No 5 for a further 15-20 minutes. Allow to cool.

6. Gently pull the buns apart to make an opening and fill with smoked salmon, cream cheese, cucumber and chicory.

AVOCADO AND CORIANDER DIP   *Serves 4*

Crispy fried potato skins, served with a variety of tasty dips, feature frequently on wine bar menus. Port and Stilton, Chilli Meat and Cheddar, Wine and Sweetcorn are all popular but this is one of my favourites.

Preparation time: 10 mins.   Cooking time: 10 mins.

2 avocados
2 tablsp garlic mayonnaise
Juice 1 lime   *(continued overleaf)*

(Avocado and Coriander Dip continued)

Salt and pepper
½ tablsp chilli sauce (optional)
2 tablsp chopped fresh coriander
Small (12 oz/340g) can asparagus tips, drained

1. Halve, peel and de-stone the avocados.

2. Mash the flesh in a small bowl.

3. Stir in the mayonnaise, lime juice, seasoning, chilli sauce and coriander.

4. Roughly chop the asparagus tips and stir them into the avocado mixture.

5. Divide the mixture between 4 individual dishes.

Serve the dip with chunks of potato which have been par-boiled for about 5 minutes then fried in hot oil for a further 5 minutes. Drain on kitchen paper. A selection of crudités also makes a good accompaniment.

11 DESSERTS

Most after work cooks I know hardly ever make sweets, relying instead on yoghurt and fresh fruit. It is of course a good choice. Different combinations of prepared fruit — fresh, dried and canned — make a welcome change from a whole apple or orange so I have included a few ideas.

The more interesting desserts are time-consuming, often expensive and do nothing for figure and health! As a treat though, it is sometimes nice to strike a happy medium between nothing and the elaborate.

Children always seem to suffer from a sweet tooth — and most men too — so hopefully some of these recipes will provide the occasional answer to plaintive cries of 'what's for afters?'.

BANANA AND ORANGE FUDGE   *Serves 4*

This syrupy fruit dessert is delicious on its own but really scrumptious spooned over ice cream. Experiment with different combinations of fruit.

Preparation time: 8 mins.   Cooking time: 10 mins.

Small knob of butter or margarine
1 tablsp flaked almonds
1 tablsp soft brown sugar
4 fl oz (100ml) orange juice
2 oranges
2 bananas

1. Melt the butter or margarine and brown the almonds for a couple of minutes.

2. Add the sugar and orange juice and boil until liquid has reduced and begins to caramelise, about 8 minutes.

3. Meanwhile remove the skin and pith from the oranges with a sharp knife. Cut the flesh into bite-size pieces.

4. Peel and slice the bananas.

5. Stir the fruit into the syrup sauce thoroughly.

ORANGE BOODLE   *Serves 4*

The combination of orange and soured cream results in a light and refreshing dessert. The mixture needs about an hour to set but can be made the day before.

Preparation time: 15 mins.   Cooking time: None.

Juice 2 large oranges
5 fl oz (150ml) carton soured cream
2 tablsp soft brown sugar
4 oz (100g) packet sponge fingers
1 small orange for decoration (optional)

1. Mix the orange juice, soured cream and sugar well together.

2. Break the sponge fingers in half and divide between four small glass sundae dishes.

3. Pour the orange and cream mixture over the sponge fingers.

4. Chill for about an hour to set. During this time occasionally press down the sponge fingers.

5. Decorate with a twist of orange if liked.

PINEAPPLE AND MELON PLATTER   *Serves 6-8*

According to research in the USA, pineapples contain rich quantities of the natural enzyme, bromelain, which helps prevent and break up dangerous blood clots. Don't go mad though, one or two pineapples a week are enough!

Preparation time: 20 mins.   Cooking time: None.

1 pineapple
1 melon
Icing sugar
Desiccated coconut

1. Cut the top and bottom off the pineapple and stand it upright. Using a sharp knife cut off the thick skin, following the natural curve of the fruit. Cut the flesh into rings and cut out the inner core.

2. Prepare the melon in the same way, removing the seeds.

3. Lay the melon and pineapple rings in a shallow serving dish and sprinkle liberally with icing sugar and desiccated coconut.

PINEAPPLE ROMANOFF   *Serves 4*

This is a simple yet impressive dessert. Strawberries and raspberries can be used in the same way.

Preparation time: 20 mins.   Cooking time: None.

1 pineapple
4 tablsp icing sugar
3 tablsp Cointreau
3 tablsp Kirsch
½ pt (300ml) double cream
Thinly pared and shredded orange rind (optional)

1. Remove the skin from the pineapple (see previous recipe). Cut fruit into quarters and remove the core. Cut flesh into bite-size chunks and place in a bowl.

2. Sprinkle on the icing sugar. Cointreau and Kirsch and mix well.

3. Whip cream until it holds its shape then fold through the pineapple mixture. Pile into individual glass dishes and decorate with finely shredded orange rind if liked.

MELON, GRAPE AND GINGER SALAD   *Serves 4-6*

I think the small Charentais melons are ideal for this dish because they have a more distinctive flavour than the other varieties.

Preparation time: 20 mins.   Cooking time: None.

2 Charentais melons
Few black and green grapes
Knob fresh ginger, peeled and coarsely grated

1. Cut the melons in half and discard the pips. Scoop out the flesh with a melon baller, or use a spoon and cut into chunks.

2. Halve the grapes and remove the pips. Time and personal preference will dictate whether you peel them.

3. Pile the fruit into individual glass dishes and top with grated ginger.

BLACK CHERRY CRUNCH

Serves 4

This is a good way to 'stretch' a can of black cherries.

Preparation time: 20 mins.   Cooking time: None.

14 oz (400g) can black cherries
5 fl oz (150ml) carton soured cream
1 tablsp black cherry jam
20 ratafia biscuits

1. De-stone the cherries.

2. Mix the soured cream and jam well together and fold into the cherries.

3. Break or cut each ratafia roughly into four and stir into the cherry mixture. Serve in individual glass dishes.

PEARS IN RED WINE

Serves 4

A classic dessert which looks attractive because the wine imparts a rosy hue to the pears. Personal preference will dictate whether to leave the pears whole, which looks more attractive for presentation purposes, or to halve and core them which is easier to eat.

Preparation time: 10 mins.   Cooking time: 30 mins.

4 good quality pears
½ pt (300ml) good full-bodied red wine
1 stick cinnamon
1 whole clove
1 tablsp soft brown sugar

1. If cooking whole pears, peel them leaving the stalks on if possible. Otherwise halve the pears and remove peel and core.

2. Poach the pears gently in the wine, cinnamon stick and clove
    for about 20 minutes. Baste and turn several times during
    cooking.

3. Remove cinnamon stick and clove and discard. Remove pears
    with a slotted spoon and arrange in a glass serving dish. Add
    the sugar to the wine and boil until syrupy, about 8 minutes.
    Pour the sauce over the pears and serve warm or cold with
    cream.

HONEYED FRUIT KEBABS

Choose a selection of fresh or canned exotic fruit and allow one
long skewer or two shorter ones per person. If liked, the prepared
fruit can be marinaded overnight in a liqueur.

Preparation time: 10-15 mins.   Cooking time: 8 mins.

Chunks of fresh pineapple
Whole apricots
Lychees
Black grapes
Bananas, cut in four
Halved and peeled peaches
Clear honey

1. Prepare the fruit, thread on skewers and spoon a little clear
    honey over.

2. Cook under a very hot grill, about 4 minutes either side until
    the honey caramelises.

ICE CREAM WITH HOT CHOCOLATE SAUCE
Serves 4

Ice cream provides a good base for a number of emergency
desserts. The melba sauce in the Peach Melba recipe also goes well
on ice cream.

Preparation time: 5 mins.   Cooking time: 8 mins.

2 oz (50g) plain chocolate
Knob butter or margarine
1 tablsp milk
1 teasp vanilla essence
4 scoops of vanilla ice cream

1. Put the chocolate and butter or margarine in a small bowl and stand it in a pan of hot water on the stove to melt.

2. Stir in the milk and vanilla essence to make a smooth creamy sauce. Do not overheat.

3. Place a scoop of ice cream in individual sundae dishes and pour over the warm sauce.

BUTTERSCOTCH SAUCE

This is another old favourite which is quickly made from stock ingredients.

Preparation time: 5 mins.   Cooking time: 5 mins.

2 oz (50g) butter or margarine
4 tablsp soft brown sugar
2 tablsp golden syrup

1. Put all three ingredients in a small saucepan and heat gently until smooth and well blended.

2. Boil for about 5 minutes until the mixture begins to thicken. Serve over vanilla ice cream.

PEACH MELBA   *Serves 4*

If possible use fresh peaches as they are much nicer. Out of season or in an emergency, use canned peach halves.

Preparation time: 8 mins.   Cooking time: 10 mins.

¼ pt (150ml) water
2 oz (50g) granulated sugar
4 tablsp raspberry jam
Juice ½ lemon
Few drops almond essence (optional)
4 scoops vanilla ice cream
2 fresh peaches, halved (and skinned if liked)

1. Put the water and sugar in a small saucepan and heat gently until the sugar has dissolved.

2. Boil rapidly for about 5 minutes until the liquid has thickened and reduced slightly.

3. Remove from heat and stir in the jam, lemon juice and almond essence.

4. Heat gently, stirring all the time until the ingredients are well blended. The sauce should just coat the back of the spoon. If it is too thin, boil for a further couple of minutes.

5. Place a scoop of ice cream in 4 sundae dishes, top with a peach half and pour over the melba sauce.

APRICOT MOUSSE   *Serves 4*

As long as you have a liquidiser this is quick and simple to make yet delicious to eat. The mousse needs time to set so is best made the night before.

Preparation time: 15 mins.   Cooking time: None.

½ oz (12.5g) packet gelatine
2 tablsp apricot juice
14 oz (397g) can apricots
½ oz (12.5g) sugar
Squeeze lemon juice
5 fl oz (150ml) carton double cream
Whipped double cream for decoration (optional)

---

3. Meanwhile, drain the pineapple, reserving the juice, and stir the liqueur into the flesh.

4. Whip the cream until it just holds its shape.

5. Stir the cream into the custard, together with the vanilla essence.

6. Cut each pastry slice into two horizontally and flatten all but one half (which will be the top) gently with the palm of your hand.

7. Sandwich together the pastry sheets, pineapple and custard mixture in alternate layers ending with the top piece of pastry.

8. Make up a thick glacé icing with the icing sugar and a little pineapple juice. Drizzle over the top of the galette. (If time is short, simply dust the top with caster sugar.)

9. Sprinkle toasted flaked almonds over the icing.

N.B. The recipe is designed for generous amounts of custard between the layers. If you feel there is too much, serve any excess separately.

APPLE CREAM BRÛLÉE   *Serves 4*

Caramelised sugar gives a crunchy, sweet topping which contrasts well with the sharp tang of apple on a thick cream base. Serve with Continental-style biscuits.

Preparation time: 10 mins.   Cooking time: 10 mins.

5 fl oz (150ml) carton double cream
8 oz (225g) carton Greek yoghurt
2 teasp vanilla essence
1 large OR 2 small crisp eating apples
Juice ½ lemon
1 teasp powdered ginger
4 tablsp demerara sugar

1. Whip the cream until it holds its shape then mix in the yoghurt and vanilla essence.

2. Pour the cream mixture into a shallow ovenproof dish.

3. Cut the apples into quarters, discard core and thinly slice the flesh.

4. Arrange the apple on top of the cream mixture and sprinkle on the lemon juice and ginger.

5. Spoon over the sugar and cook under a medium grill for about 10 minutes, until the sugar has caramelised. Serve hot or cold.

DATE AND HONEY CREAM   Serves 4

Honey acts as a natural sweetener in this recipe, and by combining the cream with yoghurt a certain amount of richness is eliminated. For quickness buy ready chopped dates.

Preparation time: 5 mins.   Cooking time: None.

5 fl oz (150ml) double cream
8 oz (225g) carton Greek yoghurt
4 oz (100g) chopped dates
Clear honey

1. Whip cream until it just holds its shape.

2. Stir in the yoghurt and dates.

3. Divide the mixture between 4 glass dishes and trickle a little honey over each.

STRAWBERRY RING   *Serves 4-6*

Choux pastry is made easily and quickly with store cupboard ingredients and is ideal for after work entertaining. If fresh strawberries are not available, use canned peach slices or black cherries. The pastry won't spoil if made the night before.

Preparation time: 15 mins.   Cooking time: 30 mins.

2 oz (50g) butter or margarine
¼ pt (150ml) water
2½ oz (65g) plain flour
Pinch salt
2 eggs, beaten
Filling
½ pt (300ml) carton double cream, whipped
Fresh strawberries or fruit of choice
Icing sugar

1. Pre-heat oven to 220°C (425°F) or Gas No 7.

2. Melt the butter or margarine in a small saucepan, add the water and bring to the boil.

3. Stir in the flour and salt all at once and beat over a low heat until the mixture leaves the side of the pan. Allow to cool for a minute or two.

4. Gradually beat in the eggs, beating well between each addition until the pastry is smooth.

5. Put dessertspoonfuls of mixture in a circle on a damp baking
    tray, making sure each spoonful touches the other.

6. Bake in the oven for 10 minutes, then turn down to 190°C
    (375°F) or Gas No 5 and bake for a further 20 minutes. Allow
    to cool.

7. Split the pastry ring in two horizontally and sandwich together
    with whipped cream and sliced strawberries. Dust the top with
    sieved icing sugar.

INDEX

OUR PUBLISHING POLICY

HOW WE CHOOSE

Our policy is to consider every deserving manuscript and we can give special editorial help where an author is an authority on his subject but an inexperienced writer. We are rigorously selective in the choice of books we publish. We set the highest standards of editorial quality and accuracy. This means that a *Paperfront* is easy to understand and delightful to read. Where illustrations are necessary to convey points of detail, these are drawn up by a subject specialist artist from our panel.

HOW WE KEEP PRICES LOW

We aim for the big seller. This enables us to order enormous print runs and achieve the lowest price for you. Unfortunately, this means that you will not find in the *Paperfront* list any titles on obscure subjects of minority interest only. These could not be printed in large enough quantities to be sold for the low price at which we offer this series. We sell almost all our *Paperfronts* at the same unit price. This saves a lot of fiddling about in our clerical departments and helps us to give you world-beating value. Under this system, the longer titles are offered at a price which we believe to be unmatched by any publisher in the world.

OUR DISTRIBUTION SYSTEM

Because of the competitive price, and the rapid turnover, *Paperfronts* are possibly the most profitable line a bookseller can handle. They are stocked by the best bookshops all over the world. It may be that your bookseller has run out of stock of a particular title. If so, he can order more from us at any time – we have a fine reputation for "same day" despatch, and we supply any order, however small (even a single copy), to any bookseller who has an account with us. We prefer you to buy from your bookseller, as this reminds him of the strong underlying public demand for *Paperfronts*. Members of the public who live in remote places, or who are housebound, or whose local bookseller is unco-operative, can order direct from us by post.

FREE

If you would like an up-to-date list of all Paperfront titles currently available, send a stamped self-addressed envelope to
ELLIOT RIGHT WAY BOOKS, BRIGHTON RD.,
LOWER KINGSWOOD, SURREY, U.K.